CAMBRIDGE LIBRARY COLLECTION

Books of enduring scholarly value

Slavery and Abolition

The books reissued in this series include accounts of historical events and movements by eye-witnesses and contemporaries, as well as landmark studies that assembled significant source materials or developed new historiographical methods. The series includes work in social, political and military history on a wide range of periods and regions, giving modern scholars ready access to influential publications of the past.

Thoughts and Sentiments on the Evil and Wicked Traffic of the Slavery and Commerce of the Human Species

In the late eighteenth century, slave labour in Britain's colonies was seen as central to world trade, and the practice was supported by prominent members of society, including the king. Ottobah Cugoano, an emancipated slave living in England, had joined the Sons of Africa, a group whose members wrote to the royal family, aristocrats and leading politicians to condemn slavery and campaign for its abolition. This work, first published in 1787 and sent to George III, was a daring attack on colonial conquest and enslavement, arguing that slaves had a moral duty to rebel against their oppressors. Widely read upon publication, it went through at least three printings that year and was translated into French, with a shorter version published in 1791. This reissue of the original work makes available an important document in the history of colonialism and slavery in the British Empire.

T0345444

Cambridge University Press has long been a pioneer in the reissuing of out-of-print titles from its own backlist, producing digital reprints of books that are still sought after by scholars and students but could not be reprinted economically using traditional technology. The Cambridge Library Collection extends this activity to a wider range of books which are still of importance to researchers and professionals, either for the source material they contain, or as landmarks in the history of their academic discipline.

Drawing from the world-renowned collections in the Cambridge University Library and other partner libraries, and guided by the advice of experts in each subject area, Cambridge University Press is using state-of-the-art scanning machines in its own Printing House to capture the content of each book selected for inclusion. The files are processed to give a consistently clear, crisp image, and the books finished to the high quality standard for which the Press is recognised around the world. The latest print-on-demand technology ensures that the books will remain available indefinitely, and that orders for single or multiple copies can quickly be supplied.

The Cambridge Library Collection brings back to life books of enduring scholarly value (including out-of-copyright works originally issued by other publishers) across a wide range of disciplines in the humanities and social sciences and in science and technology.

Thoughts and Sentiments on the Evil and Wicked Traffic of the Slavery and Commerce of the Human Species

Ottobah Cugoano

CAMBRIDGE
UNIVERSITY PRESS

CAMBRIDGE UNIVERSITY PRESS

Cambridge, New York, Melbourne, Madrid, Cape Town,
Singapore, São Paolo, Delhi, Mexico City

Published in the United States of America by Cambridge University Press, New York

www.cambridge.org
Information on this title: www.cambridge.org/9781108060196

© in this compilation Cambridge University Press 2013

This edition first published 1787
This digitally printed version 2013

ISBN 978-1-108-06019-6 Paperback

THOUGHTS

AND

SENTIMENTS

ON THE

EVIL

OF

SLAVERY.

THOUGHTS AND SENTIMENTS

ON THE

EVIL AND WICKED TRAFFIC

OF THE

SLAVERY AND COMMERCE

OF THE

HUMAN SPECIES,

HUMBLY SUBMITTED TO

The INHABITANTS of *GREAT-BRITAIN*,

BY

OTTOBAH CUGOANO,

A NATIVE of *AFRICA.*

He that stealeth a man and selleth him, or maketh merchan-
dize of him, or if he be found in his hand: then that thief
shall die.　　　　　　　　　LAW OF GOD.

L O N D O N:

PRINTED IN THE YEAR

M.DCC.LXXXVII.

GENERAL CONTENTS.

a   bourers

N. B. Since thefe Thoughts and Sentiments have been read by fome, I find a general Approbation has been given, and that the things pointed out thereby might be more effectually taken into confideration, I was requefted by fome friends to add this information concerning myfelf :— When I was kidnapped and brought away from Africa, I was then about 13 years of age, in the year of the Chriftian æra 1770; and after being about nine or ten months in the flave gang at Grenada, and about one year at different places in the Weft Indies, with Alexander Campbell, Efq; who brought me to England in the end of the year 1772, I was advifed by fome good people to get myfelf baptized, that I might not be carried away and fold again.—I was called *Steuart* by my mafter, but in order that I might embrace this ordinance, I was called *John Steuart*, and I went feveral times to Dr. Skinner, who inftructed me, and I was baptized by him, and regiftered at St. James's Church in the year 1773. Some of my fellow-fervants, who affifted me in this, got themfelves turned away for it ; I have only put my African name to the title of the book.—When I was brought away from Africa, my father and relations were then chief men in the kingdom of Agimaque and Affinee; but what they may be now, or whether dead or alive, I know not. I wifh to go back as foon as I can hear any proper fecurity and fafe conveyance can be found ; and I wait to hear how it fares with the Black People fent to Sierra Leona. But it is my higheft wifh and earneft prayer to God, that fome encouragement could be given to fend able fchool mafters, and intelligent minifters, who would be faithful and able to teach the Chriftian religion. This would be doing great good to the Africans, and be a kind reftitution for the great injuries that they have fuffered. But ftill I fear no good can be done near any of the European fettlements, while fuch a horrible and infernal traffic of flavery is carried on by them. Wherever the foot of man can go, at the forts and garrifons it would feem to be wrote with thefe words——

O earth! O fea! cover not thou the blood of the poor negro flaves.

THOUGHTS and SENTIMENTS

ON THE

EVIL of SLAVERY.

One law, and one manner shall be for you, and for the stranger that sojourneth with you; and therefore, all things whatsoever ye would that men should do to you, do ye even so to them.

Numb. xv. 16.—Math. vii. 12.

AS several learned gentlemen of distinguished abilities, as well as eminent for their great humanity, liberality and candour, have written various essays against that infamous traffic of the African Slave Trade, carried on with the West-India planters and merchants, to the great shame and disgrace of all Christian nations wherever it is admitted in any of their territories, or in any place or situation amongst them; it cannot be amiss that I should thankfully acknowledge these truly worthy and humane gentlemen with the warmest sense of gratitude, for their beneficent and laudable endeavours towards a total suppression of that infamous and iniquitous traffic of stealing, kid-napping, buying, selling, and cruelly enslaving men!

B   Those

Thofe who have endeavoured to reftore to their fellow-creatures the common rights of nature, of which efpecially the poor unfortunate Black People have been fo unjuftly deprived, cannot fail in meeting with the applaufe of all good men, and the approbation of that which will for ever redound to their honor; they have the warrant of that which is divine: *Open thy mouth, judge righteoufly, plead the caufe of the poor and needy; for the liberal devifeth liberal things, and by liberal things fhall ftand.* And they can fay with the pious Job, *Did not I weep for him that was in trouble; was not my foul grieved for the poor?*

The kind exertions of many benevolent and humane gentlemen, againft the iniquitous traffic of flavery and oppreffion, has been attended with much good to many, and muft redound with great honor to themfelves, to humanity and their country; their laudable endeavours have been productive of the moft beneficent effects in preventing that favage barbarity from taking place in free countries at home. In this, as well as in many other refpects, there is one clafs of people (whofe virtues of probity and humanity are well known) who are worthy of univerfal approbation and imitation, becaufe, like men of honor and humanity, they have jointly agreed to carry on no flavery and favage barbarity among them; and, fince the laft war, fome mitigation of flavery has been obtained in fome refpective diftricts of America, though not in proportion to their own vaunted claims of freedom; but it is to be hoped, that they will yet go on to make a further and greater reformation. However, notwithftanding all that has been done and written againft it, that brutifh barbarity, and unparalelled injuftice, is ftill carried

ried on to a very great extent in the colonies, and with an avidity as infidious, cruel and oppreffive as ever. The longer that men continue in the practice of evil and wickednefs, they grow the more abandoned; for nothing in hiftory can equal the barbarity and cruelty of the tortures and murders committed under various pretences in modern flavery, except the annals of the Inquifition and the bloody edicts of Popifh maffacres.

It is therefore manifeft, that fomething elfe ought yet to be done; and what is required, is evidently the incumbent duty of all men of enlightened underftanding, and of every man that has any claim or affinity to the name of Chriftian, that the bafe treatment which the African Slaves undergo, ought to be abolifhed; and it is moreover evident, that the whole, or any part of that iniquitous traffic of flavery, can no where, or in any degree, be admitted, but among thofe who muft eventually refign their own claim to any degree of fenfibility and humanity, for that of barbarians and ruffians.

But it would be needlefs to arrange an hiftory of all the bafe treatment which the African Slaves are fubjected to, in order to fhew the exceeding wickednefs and evil of that infidious traffic, as the whole may eafily appear in every part, and at every view, to be wholly and totally inimical to every idea of juftice, equity, reafon and humanity. What I intend to advance againft that evil, criminal and wicked traffic of enflaving men, are only fome Thoughts and Sentiments which occur to me, as being obvious from the Scriptures of Divine Truth, or fuch arguments as are chiefly deduced from thence, with other fuch obfervations as I have been able to collect. Some

of

of thefe obfervations may lead into a larger field
of confideration, than that of the African Slave
Trade alone; but thofe caufes from wherever
they originate, and become the production of
flavery, the evil effects produced by it, muft fhew
that its origin and fource is of a wicked and criminal nature.

No neceffity, or any fituation of men, however
poor, pitiful and wretched they may be, can warrant them to rob others, or oblige them to become thieves, becaufe they are poor, miferable
and wretched: But the robbers of men, the kidnappers, enfnarers and flave-holders, who take
away the common rights and privileges of others
to fupport and enrich themfelves, are univerfally
thofe pitiful and deteftable wretches; for the en-
fnaring of others, and taking away their liberty
by flavery and oppreffion, is the worft kind of
robbery, as moft oppofite to every precept and
injunction of the Divine Law, and contrary to
that command which enjoins that *all men fhould
love their neighbours as themfelves*, and *that they
fhould do unto others, as they would that men fhould
do to them*. As to any other laws that flave-
holders may make among themfelves, as refpecting flaves, they can be of no better kind, nor give
them any better character, than what is implied
in the common report—that there may be fome
honefty among thieves. This may feem a harfh
comparifon, but the parallel is fo coincident that,
I muft fay, I can find no other way of expref-
fing my Thoughts and Sentiments, without making ufe of fome harfh words and comparifons
againft the carriers on of fuch abandoned wickednefs. But, in this little undertaking, I muft
humbly hope the impartial reader will excufe fuch
defects

defects as may arife from want of better education; and as to the refentment of thofe who can
lay their cruel lafh upon the backs of thoufands,
for a thoufand times lefs crimes than writing
againft their enormous wickednefs and brutal
avarice, is what I may be fure to meet with.

However, it cannot but be very difcouraging
to a man of my complexion in fuch an attempt
as this, to meet with the evil afperfions of fome
men, who fay, " That an African is not entitled
" to any competent degree of knowledge, or ca-
" pable of imbibing any fentiments of probity;
" and that nature defigned him for fome inferior
" link in the chain, fitted only to be a flave."
But when I meet with thofe who make no fcruple
to deal with the human fpecies, as with the beafts
of the earth, I muft think them not only brutifh,
but wicked and bafe; and that their afperfions
are infidious and falfe: And if fuch men can boaft
of greater degrees of knowledge, than any African
is entitled to, I fhall let them enjoy all the advantages of it unenvied, as I fear it confifts only
in a greater fhare of infidelity, and that of a
blacker kind than only fkin deep.   And if their
complexion be not what I may fuppofe, it is at
leaft the neareft in refemblance to an infernal hue.
A good man will neither fpeak nor do as a bad
man will; but if a man is bad, it makes no difference whether he be a black or a white devil.

By fome of fuch complexion, as whether black
or white it matters not, I was early fnatched away
from my native country, with about eighteen or
twenty more boys and girls, as we were playing
in a field.   We lived but a few days journey from
the coaft where we were kid-napped, and as we
were decoyed and drove along, we were foon con-

B 3   ducted

ducted to a factory, and from thence, in the fashionable way of traffic, configned to Grenada. Perhaps it may not be amifs to give a few remarks, as fome account of myfelf, in this tranfpofition of captivity.

I was born in the city of Agimaque, on the coaft of Fantyn; my father was a companion to the chief in that part of the country of Fantee, and when the old king died I was left in his houfe with his family; foon after I was fent for by his nephew, Ambro Accafa, who fucceeded the old king in the chiefdom of that part of Fantee known by the name of Agimaque and Affinee. I lived with his children, enjoying peace and tranquillity, about twenty moons, which, according to their way of reckoning time, is two years. I was fent for to vifit an uncle, who lived at a confiderable diftance from Agimaque. The firft day after we fet out we arrived at Affinee, and the third day at my uncle's habitation, where I lived about three months, and was then thinking of returning to my father and young companion at Agimaque; but by this time I had got well acquainted with fome of the children of my uncle's hundreds of relations, and we were fome days too venturfome in going into the woods to gather fruit and catch birds, and fuch amufements as pleafed us. One day I refufed to go with the reft, being rather apprehenfive that fomething might happen to us; till one of my play-fellows faid to me, becaufe you belong to the great men, you are afraid to venture your carcafe, or elfe of the *bounfam*, which is the devil. This enraged me fo much, that I fet a refolution to join the reft, and we went into the woods as ufual; but we had not been above two hours before our troubles began,
                                                    when

when feveral great ruffians came upon us fuddenly, and faid we had committed a fault againſt
their lord, and we muſt go and anſwer for it ourfelves before him.

Some of us attempted in vain to run away, but
piſtols and cutlaſſes were foon introduced, threat-
ening, that if we offered to ſtir we ſhould all lie
dead on the ſpot. One of them pretended to be
more friendly than the reſt, and faid, that he
would ſpeak to their lord to get us clear, and defired that we ſhould follow him; we were then
immediately divided into different parties, and
drove after him. We were foon led out of the
way which we knew, and towards the evening, as
we came in fight of a town, they told us that this
great man of theirs lived there, but pretended it
was too late to go and fee him that night. Next
morning there came three other men, whofe language differed from ours, and ſpoke to fome of
thofe who watched us all the night, but he that
pretended to be our friend with the great man,
and fome others, were gone away. We aſked our
keepers what thefe men had been faying to them,
and they anſwered, that they had been aſking
them, and us together, to go and feaſt with them
that day, and that we muſt put off feeing the
great man till after; little thinking that our
doom was fo nigh, or that thefe villains meant to
feaſt on us as their prey. We went with them
again about half a day's journey, and came to a
great multitude of people, having different mufic
playing; and all the day after we got there, we
were very merry with the mufic, dancing and
finging. Towards the evening, we were again
perfuaded that we could not get back to where
the great man lived till next day; and when bed-
time

time came, we were feparated into different houfes with different people. When the next morning came, I afked for the men that brought me there, and for the reft of my companions; and I was told that they were gone to the fea fide to bring home fome rum, guns and powder, and that fome of my companions were gone with them and that fome were gone to the fields to do fomething or other. This gave me ftrong fufpicion that there was fome treachery in the cafe, and I began to think that my hopes of returning home again were all over. I foon became very uneafy, not knowing what to do, and refufed to eat or drink for whole days together, till the man of the houfe told me that he would do all in his power to get me back to my uncle; then I eat a little fruit with him, and had fome thoughts that I fhould be fought after, as I would be then miffing at home about five or fix days. I enquired every day if the men had come back, and for the reft of my companions, but could get no anfwer of any fatis-faction. I was kept about fix days at this man's houfe, and in the evening there was another man came and talked with him a good while, and I heard the one fay to the other he muft go, and the other faid the fooner the better; that man came out and told me that he knew my relations at Agimaque, and that we muft fet out to-morrow morning, and he would convey me there. Ac-cordingly we fet out next day, and travelled till dark, when we came to a place where we had fome fupper and flept. He carried a large bag with fome gold duft, which he faid he had to buy fome goods at the fea fide to take with him to Agimaque. Next day we travelled on, and in the evening came to a town, where I faw feveral
white

white people, which made me afraid that they would eat me, according to our notion as children in the inland parts of the country. This made me reft very uneafy all the night, and next morning I had fome victuals brought, defiring me to eat and make hafte, as my guide and kid-napper told me that he had to go to the caftle with fome company that were going there, as he had told me before, to get fome goods. After I was ordered out, the horrors I foon faw and felt, cannot be well defcribed; I faw many of my miferable countrymen chained two and two, fome hand-cuffed, and fome with their hands tied behind. We were conducted along by a guard, and when we arrived at the caftle, I afked my guide what I was brought there for, he told me to learn the ways of the *browfow*, that is the white faced people. I faw him take a gun, a piece of cloth, and fome lead for me, and then he told me that he muft now leave me there, and went off. This made me cry bitterly, but I was foon conducted to a prifon, for three days, where I heard the groans and cries of many, and faw fome of my fellow-captives. But when a veffel arrived to conduct us away to the fhip, it was a moft horrible fcene; there was nothing to be heard but rattling of chains, fmacking of whips, and the groans and cries of our fellow-men. Some would not ftir from the ground, when they were lafhed and beat in the moft horrible manner. I have forgot the name of this infernal fort; but we were taken in the fhip that came for us, to another that was ready to fail from Cape Coaft. When we were put into the fhip, we faw feveral black merchants coming on board, but we were all drove into our holes, and not fuffered to fpeak to any of them. In this fituation

we

we continued feveral days in fight of our native land; but I could find no good perfon to give any information of my fituation to Accafa at Agima- que. And when we found ourfelves at laft taken away, death was more preferable than life, and a plan was concerted amongft us, that we might burn and blow up the fhip, and to perifh all to- gether in the flames; but we were betrayed by one of our own countrywomen, who flept with fome of the head men of the fhip, for it was com- mon for the dirty filthy failors to take the African women and lie upon their bodies; but the men were chained and pent up in holes. It was the women and boys which were to burn the fhip, with the approbation and groans of the reft; though that was prevented, the difcovery was likewife a cruel bloody fcene.

But it would be needlefs to give a defcription of all the horrible fcenes which we faw, and the bafe treatment which we met with in this dread- ful captive fituation, as the fimilar cafes of thou- fands, which fuffer by this infernal traffic, are well known. Let it fuffice to fay, that I was thus loft to my dear indulgent parents and relations, and they to me. All my help was cries and tears, and thefe could not avail; nor fuffered long, till one fucceeding woe, and dread, fwelled up another. Brought from a ftate of innocence and freedom, and, in a barbarous and cruel manner, conveyed to a ftate of horror and flavery : This abandoned fituation may be eafier conceived than defcribed. From the time that I was kid-napped and con- ducted to a factory, and from thence in the brut- ifh, bafe, but fafhionable way of traffic, confign- ed to Grenada, the grievous thoughts which I then felt, ftill pant in my heart; though my fears and

and tears have long fince fubfided. And yet it is ftill grievous to think that thoufands more have fuffered in fimilar and greater diftrefs, under the hands of barbarous robbers, and mercilefs tafk-mafters; and that many even now are fuffering in all the extreme bitternefs of grief and woe, that no language can defcribe The cries of fome, and the fight of their mifery, may be feen and heard afar; but the deep founding groans of thoufands, and the great fadnefs of their mifery and woe, under the heavy load of oppreffions and calamities inflicted upon them, are fuch as can only be diftinctly known to the ears of Jehovah Sabaoth.

This Lord of Hofts, in his great Providence, and in great mercy to me, made a way for my deliverance from Grenada.—Being in this dread-ful captivity and horrible flavery, without any hope of deliverance, for about eight or nine months, beholding the moft dreadful fcenes of mifery and cruelty, and feeing my miferable com-panions often cruelly lafhed, and as it were cut to pieces, for the moft trifling faults; this made me often tremble and weep, but I efcaped better than many of them. For eating a piece of fugar-cane, fome were cruelly lafhed, or ftruck over the face to knock their teeth out. Some of the ftouter ones, I fuppofe often reproved, and grown hardened and ftupid with many cruel beatings and lafhings, or perhaps faint and preffed with hunger and hard labour, were often committing trefpaffes of this kind, and when detected, they met with exemplary punifhment. Some told me they had their teeth pulled out to deter others, and to pre-vent them from eating any cane in future. Thus feeing my miferable companions and countrymen
in

in this pitiful, diftreffed and horrible fituation, with all the brutifh bafenefs and barbarity attending it, could not but fill my little mind with horror and indignation. But I muft own, to the fhame of my own countrymen, that I was firft kid-napped and betrayed by fome of my own complexion, who were the firft caufe of my exile and flavery; but if there were no buyers there would be no fellers. So far as I can remember, fome of the Africans in my country keep flaves, which they take in war, or for debt; but thofe which they keep are well fed, and good care taken of them, and treated well; and, as to their cloathing, they differ according to the cuftom of the country. But I may fafely fay, that all the poverty and mifery that any of the inhabitants of Africa meet with among themfelves, is far inferior to thofe inhofpitable regions of mifery which they meet with in the Weft-Indies, where their hard-hearted overfeers have neither regard to the laws of God, nor the life of their fellow-men.

Thanks be to God, I was delivered from Grenada, and that horrid brutal flavery.—A gentleman coming to England, took me for his fervant, and brought me away, where I foon found my fituation become more agreeable. After coming to England, and feeing others write and read, I had a ftrong defire to learn, and getting what affiftance I could, I applied myfelf to learn reading and writing, which foon became my recreation, pleafure, and delight; and when my mafter perceived that I could write fome, he fent me to a proper fchool for that purpofe to learn. Since, I have endeavoured to improve my mind in reading, and have fought to get all the intelligence I could, in my fituation of life, towards the ftate of

my

my brethren and countrymen in complexion, and
of the miferable fituation of thofe who are barbaroufly fold into captivity, and unlawfully held
in flavery.

But, among other obfervations, one great duty
I owe to Almighty God, (the thankful acknow-
ledgement I would not omit for any confideration) that, although I have been brought away
from my native country, in that torrent of robbery and wickednefs, thanks be to God for his
good providence towards me; I have both obtained liberty, and acquired the great advantages
of fome little learning, in being able to read and
write, and, what is ftill infinitely of greater advantage, I truft, to know fomething of HIM *who
is that God whofe providence rules over all, and who
is the only Potent One that rules in the nations over
the children of men. It is unto Him, who is the
Prince of the Kings of the earth, that I would give
all thanks.* And, in fome manner, I may fay
with Jofeph, as he did with refpect to the evil
intention of his brethren, when they fold him
into Egypt, that whatever evil intentions and bad
motives thofe infidious robbers had in carrying
me away from my native country and friends, I
truft, was what the Lord intended for my good.
In this refpect, I am highly indebted to many of
the good people of England for learning and principles unknown to the people of my native country.   But, above all, what have I obtained from
the Lord God of Hofts, the God of the Chriftians! in that divine revelation of the only true
God, and the Saviour of men, what a treafure of
wifdom and bleffings are involved? How wonderful is the divine goodnefs difplayed in thofe
invaluable books the Old and New Teftaments,
that

that ineftimable compilation of books, the Bible?
And, O what a treafure to have, and one of the
greateft advantages to be able to read therein,
and a divine blefling to underftand * !

But, to return to my fubject, I begin with the
Curfory Remarker. This man ftiles himfelf a
friend to the Weft-India colonies and their inhabitants, like Demetrius, the filverfmith, a man
of fome confiderable abilities, feeing their craft
in danger, a craft, however, not fo innocent and
juftifiable as the making of fhrines for Diana,
though that was bafe and wicked enough to enflave the minds of men with fuperftition and idolatry; but his craft, and the gain of thofe craftfmen, confifts in the enflaving both foul and body
to the cruel idolatry, and moft abominable fervice and flavery, to the idol of curfed avarice:
And as he finds fome difcoveries of their wicked
traffic held up in a light where truth and facts are
fo clearly feen, as none but the moft defperate
villain would dare to obftruct or oppofe, he therefore fallies forth with all the defperation of an

* The juftly celebrated Dr. Young, in recommending this
divine book of heavenly wifdom to the giddy and thoughtlefs
world, in his Night Thoughts, has the following elegant
lines :

> Perhaps thou'dft langh but at thine own expence,
> This counfel ftrange fhould I prefume to give ;
> Retire and read thy Bible to be gay ;
> There truths abound of fov'reign aid to peace.
> Ah, do not prize it lefs becaufe infpired.
> Read and revere the facred page ; a page,
> Where triumphs immortality ; a page,
> Which not the whole creation could produce ;
> Which not the conflagration fhall deftroy ;
> In nature's ruin not one letter's loft,
> 'Tis printed in the mind of gods for ever,
> Angels and men affent to what I fing !

Utopian

Utopian affailant, to tell lies by a virulent contradiction of facts, and with falfe afperfions endeavour to calumniate the worthy and judicious effayeft of that difcovery, a man, whofe character is irreproachable. By thus artfully fuppofing, if he could bring the reputation of the author, who has difcovered fo much of their iniquitous traffic, into difpute, his work would fall and be lefs regarded. However, this virulent craftfman has done no great merit to his caufe and the credit of that infamous craft; at the appearance of truth, his underftanding has got the better of his avarice and infidelity, fo far, as to draw the following conceffion: " I fhall not be fo far mifunder-
" ftood, by the candid and judicious part of man-
" kind, as to be ranked among the advocates of
" flavery, as I moft fincerely join Mr. Ramfay *,
" and every other man of fenfibility, in hoping
" the bleffings of freedom will, in due time, be
" equally diffufed over the whole globe."

By this, it would feem that he was a little afhamed of his craftfmen, and would not like to be ranked or appear amongft them. But as long as there are any hopes of gain to be made by that infidious craft, he can join with them well enough, and endeavour to juftify them in that moft abandoned traffic of buving, felling, and enflaving men. He finds fault with a plan for punifhing robbers, thieves and vagabonds, who diftrefs their neighbours by their thrift, robbery and plunder, without regarding any laws human or divine, except the rules of their own fraternity, and in that

---

* The worthy and judicious author of " An Effay on the
" Treatment and Converfion of the African Slaves in the
" Britifh Sugar Colonies.

cafe,

cafe, according to the proverb, there may be fome honor among thieves; but thefe are the only people in the world that ought to fuffer fome punifhment, imprifonment or flavery; their external complexion, whether black or white, fhould be no excufe for them to do evil. Being aware of this, perhaps he was afraid that fome of his friends, the great and opulent banditti of flaveholders in the weftern part of the world, might be found guilty of more atrocious and complicated crimes, than even thofe of the highwaymen, the robberies and the petty larcenies committed in England. Therefore, to make the beft of this fad dilemma, he brings in a ludicrous invective comparifon that it would be " an event which " would undoubtedly furnifh a new and pleafant " compartment to that well known and moft de- " lectable print, call'd, *The world turn'd up fide* " *down*, in which the cook is roafted by the pig, " the man faddled by the horfe," &c. If he means that the complicated banditties of pirates, thieves, robbers, oppreffors and enflavers of men, are thofe cooks and men that would be roafted and faddled, it certainly would be no unpleafant fight to fee them well roafted, faddled and bridled too; and no matter by whom, whether he terms them pigs, horfes or affes. But there is not much likelihood of this filly monkeyifh comparifon as yet being verified, in bringing the opulent pirates and thieves to condign punifhment, fo that he could very well bring it in to turn it off with a grin. However, to make ufe of his words, it would be a moft delectable fight, when thieves and robbers get the upper fide of the world, to fee them turned down; and I fhould not interrupt his mirth, to fee him laugh at his

own

own invective monkeyifh comparifon as long as
he pleafes.

But again, when he draws a comparifon of the
many hardfhips that the poor in Great-Britain
and Ireland labour under, as well as many of
thofe in ot er countries ; that their various diftreffes are worfe than the Weft India flaves—It
may be true, in part, that fome of them fuffer
greater hardfhips than many of the flaves; but,
bad as it is, the pooreft in England would not
change their fituation for that of flaves. And
there may be fome mafters, under various circumftances, worfe off than their fervants; but
they would not change their own fituation for
theirs : Nor as little would a rich man wifh to
change his fituation of affluence, for that of a
beggar : and fo, likewife, no freeman, however
poor and diftreffing his fituation may be, would
refign his liberty for that of a flave, in the fituation of a horfe or a dog.   The cafe of the poor,
whatever their hardfhips may be, in free countries, is widely different from that of the Weft-
India flaves.   For the flaves, like animals, are
bought and fold, and dealt with as their capri-
cious owners may think fit, even in torturing and
tearing them to pieces, and wearing them out
with hard labour, hunger and oppreffion; and
fhould the death of a flave enfue by fome other
more violent way than that which is commonly
the death of thoufands, and tens of thoufands in
the end, the haughty tyrant, in that cafe, has
only to pay a fmall fine for the murder and death
of his flave.   The brute creation in general may
fare better than man, and fome dogs may refufe
the crumbs that the diftreffed poor would be glad
of ; but the nature and fituation of man is far fu-

C   perior

perior to that of beafts; and, in like manner, whatever circumftances poor freemen may be in, their fituation is much fuperior, beyond any proportion, to that of the hardfhips and cruelty of modern flavery. But where can the fituation of any freeman be fo bad as that of a flave; or, could fuch be found, or even worfe, as he would have it, what would the comparifon amount to? Would it plead for his craft of flavery and oppreffion? Or, rather, would it not cry aloud for fome redrefs, and what every well regulated fociety of men ought to hear and confider, that none fhould fuffer want or be oppreffed among them? And this feems to be pointed out by the circumftances which he defcribes; that it is the great duty, and ought to be the higheft ambition of all governors, to order and eftablifh fuch policy, and in fuch a wife manner, that every thing fhould be fo managed, as to be conducive to the moral, temporal and eternal welfare of every individual from the loweft degree to the higheft; and the confequence of this would be, the harmony, happinefs and good profperity of the whole community.

But this crafty author has alfo, in defence of his own or his employer's craft in the Britifh Weft-India flavery, given fundry comparifons and defcriptions of the treatment of flaves in the French iflands and fettlements in the Weft Indies and America. And, contrary to what is the true cafe, he would have it fuppofed that the treatment of the flaves in the former, is milder than the latter; but even in this, unwarily for his own craft of flavery, all that he has advanced, can only add matter for its confutation, and ferve to heighten the ardour and wifh of every

generous

generous mind, that the whole fhould be abolifhed. An equal degree of enormity found in one place, cannot juftify crimes of as great or greater enormity committed in another. The various depredations committed by robbers and plunderers, on different parts of the globe, may not be all equally alike bad, but their evil and malignancy, in every appearance and fhape, can only hold up to view the juft obfervation, that

Virtue herfelf hath fuch peculiar mein,
Vice, to be hated, needs but to be feen.

The farther and wider that the difcovery and knowledge of fuch an enormous evil, as the bafe and villainous treatment and flavery which the poor unfortunate Black People meet with, is fpread and made known, the cry for juftice, even virtue lifting up her voice, muft rife the louder and higher, for the fcale of equity and juftice to be lifted up in their defence. *And doth not wifdom cry, and underftanding put forth her voice?* But who will regard the voice and hearken to the cry? Not the fneaking advocates for flavery, though a little afhamed of their craft; like the monftrous crocodile weeping over their prey with fine conceffions (while gorging their own rapacious appetite) to hope for univerfal freedom taking place over the globe. Not thofe inebriated with avarice and infidelity, who hold in defiance every regard due to the divine law, and who endeavour all they can to deftroy and take away the natural and common rights and privileges of men. Not the infolent and crafty author for flavery and oppreffion, who would have us to believe, that the benign command of God in appointing the feventh day for a fabbath of reft for the good purpofes of our prefent and eternal wel-

fare,

fare, is not to be regarded. He will exclaim againſt the teachers of obedience to it ; and tells us, that the poor, and the oppreſſed, and the heavy burdened ſlave, ſhould not lay down his load that day, but appropriate theſe hours of ſacred reſt to labour in ſome bit of uſeful ground. His own words are, " to dedicate the unappro-" priated hours of Sunday to the cultivation of " this uſeful ſpot, he is brought up to believe " would be the worſt of ſins, and that the ſab-" bath is a day of abſolute and univerſal reſt is a " truth he hears frequently inculcated by the cu-" rate of the pariſh," &c. But after bringing it about in this round-about way and manner, whatever the curate has to ſay of it as a truth, he would have us by no means to regard. This may ſerve as a ſpecimen of his crafty and deteſtable production, where infidelity, falſe aſperſions, virulent calumnies, and lying contradictions abound throughout. I ſhall only refer him to that deſcription which he meant for another, as moſt applicable and beſt ſuited for himſelf; and ſo long as he does not renounce his craft, as well as to be ſomewhat aſhamed of his craftſmen and their inſenſibility, he may thus ſtand as deſcribed by himſelf : " A man of warm imagination (but " ſtrange infatuated unfeeling ſenſibility) to paint " things not as they really are, but as his rooted " prejudices repreſent them, and even to ſhut his " eyes againſt the convictions afforded him by his " own ſenſes."

But ſuch is the inſenſibility of men, when their own craft of gain is advanced by the ſlavery and oppreſſion of others, that after all the laudable exertions of the truly virtuous and humane, towards extending the beneficence of liberty and freedom

freedom to the much degraded and unfortunate
Africans, which is the common right and privi-
lege of all men, in every thing that is juſt, lawful and confiſtent, we find the principles of juſtice
and equity, not only oppoſed, and every duty in
religion and humanity left unregarded ; but that
unlawful traffic of dealing with our fellow-creatures, as with the beaſts of the earth, ſtill carried
on with as great aſſiduity as ever; and that the
inſidious piracy of procuring and holding ſlaves
is countenanced and ſupported by the government of ſundry Chriſtian nations.   This ſeems to
be the faſhionable way of getting riches, but very
diſhonourable ; in doing this, the ſlave-holders
are meaner and baſer than the African ſlaves. for
while they ſubject and reduce them to a degree
with brutes, they ſeduce themſelves to a degree
with devils.

   " Some pretend that the Africans, in general,
" are a ſet of poor, ignorant, diſperſed, unſoci-
" able people ; and that they think it no crime to
" ſell one another, and even their own wives and
" children ; therefore they bring them away to a
" ſituation where many of them may arrive to a
" better ſtate than ever they could obtain in their
" own native country."   This ſpecious pretence
is without any ſhadow of juſtice and truth, and,
if the argument was even true, it could afford no
juſt and warrantable matter for any ſociety of
men to hold ſlaves.   But the argument is falſe ;
there can be no ignorance, diſperſion, or unſoci-
ableneſs ſo found among them, which can be
made better by bringing them away to a ſtate of
a degree equal to that of a cow or a horſe.

   But let their ignorance in ſome things (in
which the Europeans have greatly the advantage
of

of them) be what it will, it is not the intention of thofe who bring them away to make them better by it ; nor is the defign of flave-holders of any other intention, but that they may ferve them as a kind of engines and beafts of burden ; that their own eafe and profit may be advanced, by a fet of poor helplefs men and women whom they defpife and rank with brutes, and keep them in perpetual flavery, both themfelves and children, and merciful death is the only releafe from their toil. By the benevolence of fome, a few may get their liberty, and by their own induftry and ingenuity, may acquire fome learning, mechanical trades, or ufeful bufinefs ; and fome may be brought away by different gentlemen to free countries, where they get their liberty but no thanks to flave-holders for it. But amongft thofe who get their liberty, like all other ignorant men, are generally more corrupt in their morals, than they poffibly could have been amongft their own people in Africa; for, being moftly amongft the wicked and apoftate Chriftians, they fooner learn their oaths and blafphemies, and their evil ways, than any thing elfe. Some few, indeed, may eventually arrive at fome knowledge of the Chriftian religion, and the great advantages of it. Such was the cafe of Ukawfaw Groniofaw, an African prince, who lived in England. He was a long time in a ftate of great poverty and diftrefs, and muft have died at one time for want, if a good and charitable Attorney had not fupported him. He was long after in a very poor ftate, but he would not have given his faith in the Chriftian religion, in exchange for all the kingdoms of Africa, if they could have been given to him, in place of his poverty, for it.

And

And fuch was A. Morrant in America. When a boy, he could ftroll away into a defart, and prefer the fociety of wild beafts to the abfurd Chriftianity of his mother's houfe. He was conducted to the king of the Cherokees, who, in a miraculous manner, was induced by him to embrace the Chriftian faith. This Morrant was in the Britifh fervice laft war, and his royal convert, the king of the Cherokee Indians, accompanied General Clinton at the fiege of Charles-Town.

Thefe, and all fuch, I hope thoufands, as meet with the knowledge and grace of the Divine clemency, are brought forth quite contrary to the end and intention of all flavery, and, in general, of all flave holders too. And fhould it pleafe the Divine goodnefs to vifit fome of the poor dark Africans, even in the brutal ftall of flavery, and from thence to inftal them among the princes of his grace, and to inveft them with a robe of honor that will hang about their necks for ever; but who can then fuppofe, that it will be well pleafing unto him to find them fubjected there in that dejected ftate? Or can the flave-holders think that the Univerfal Father and Sovereign of Mankind will be well pleafed with them, for the brutal tranfgreffion of his law, in bowing down the necks of thofe to the yoke of their cruel bondage? Sovereign goodnefs may eventually vifit fome men even in a ftate of flavery, but their flavery is not the caufe of that event and benignity; and therefore, fhould fome event of good ever happen to fome men fubjected to flavery, that can plead nothing for men to do evil that good may come; and fhould it apparently happen from thence, it is neither fought for nor defigned by the enflavers of men. But the whole bufinefs of

flavery

flavery is an evil of the firſt magnitude, and a moſt horrible iniquity to traffic with ſlaves and fouls of men ; and an evil. forry I am, that it ſtill ſubſiſts, and more aſtoniſhing to think, that it is an iniquity committed amongſt Chriſtians, and contrary to all the genuine principles of Chriſtianity, and yet carried on by men denominated thereby.

In a Chriſtian æra, in a land where Chriſtianity is planted, where every one might expeͨt to behold the flouriſhing growth of every virtue, extending their harmonious branches with univerſal philanthropy wherever they came ; but, on the contrary, almoſt nothing elſe is to be ſeen abroad but the bramble of ruffians, barbarians and ſlave-holders, grown up to a powerful luxuriance in wickedneſs. I cannot but wiſh, for the honor of Chriſtianity, that the bramble grown up amongſt them, was known to the heathen nations by a different name, for ſure the depredators, robbers and enſnarers of men can never be Chriſtians, but ought to be held as the abhorence of all men, and the abomination of all mankind, whether Chriſtians or heathens. Every man of any ſenſibility, whether he be a Chriſtian or an heathen, if he has any diſcernment at all, muſt think. that for any man, or any claſs of men, to deal with their fellow-creatures as with the beaſts of the field ; or to account them as ſuch, however ignorant they may be, and in whatever ſituation, or wherever they may find them, and whatever country or complexion they may be of, that thoſe men, who are the procurers and holders of ſlaves, are the greateſt villains in the world. And ſurely thoſe men muſt be loſt to all ſenſibility themſelves, who can think that the ſtealing, robbing,

robbing, enflaving, and murdering of men can
be no crimes; but the holders of men in flavery
are at the head of all thefe oppreffions and crimes.
And, therefore, however unfenfible they may be
of it now, and however long they may laugh at
the calamity of others, if they do not repent of
their evil way, and the wickednefs of their do-
ings. by keeping and holding their fellow creatures in flavery, and trafficking with them as
with the brute creation, and to give up and furrender that evil traffic, with an awful abhorrence
of it, that this may be averred, if they do not,
and if they can think, they muft and cannot
otherwife but expect in one day at laft, to meet
with the full ftroke of the long fufpended vengeance of heaven, when death will cut them
down to a ftate as mean as that of the moft ab-
jected flave, and to a very eminent danger of a
far more dreadful fate hereafter, when they have
the juft reward of their iniquities to meet with.

And now, as to the Africans being difperfed
and unfociable, if it was fo, that could be no warrant for the Europeans to enflave them; and even
though they may have many different feuds and
bad practices among them, the continent of
Africa is of vaft extent, and the numerous inhabitants are divided into feveral kingdoms and
principalities, which are governed by their refpective kings and princes, and thofe are abfolutely maintained by their free fubjects. Very
few nations make flaves of any of thofe under
their government; but fuch as are taken prifoners of war from their neighbours, are generally
kept in that ftate, until they can exchange and
difpofe of them otherwife; and towards the weft
coaft they are generally procured for the European

ropean market, and fold. They have a great averfion to murder, or even in taking away the lives of thofe which they judge guilty of crimes; and, therefore, they prefer difpofing of them otherwife better than killing them *. This gives their merchants and procurers of flaves a power to travel a great way into the interior parts of the country to buy fuch as are wanted to be difpofed of. Thefe flave-procurers are a fet of as great villains as any in the world. They often fteal and kidnap many more than they buy at firft if they can meet with them by the way; and they have only their certain boundaries to go to, and fell them from one to another; fo that if they are fought after and detected, the thieves are feldom found, and the others only plead that they bought them fo and fo. Thefe kid nappers and flave-procurers, called merchants, are a fpecies of African villains, which are greatly corrupted, and even viciated by their intercourfe with the Europeans; but, wicked and barbarous as they certainly are, I can hardly think, if they knew what horrible barbarity they were fending their fellow-creatures to, that they would do it. But the artful Europeans have fo deceived them, that they are bought by their inventions of merchandize, and beguiled into it by their artifice; for the Europeans, at their factories, in fome various manner, have always kept fome as fervants to them, and with gaudy cloaths, in a

* It may be true, that fome of the flaves tranfported from Africa, may have committed crimes in their own country, that require fome flavery as a punifhment; but, according to the laws of equity and juftice, they ought to become free, as foon as their labour has paid for their purchafe in the Weft-Indies or elfewhere.

gay manner, as decoy ducks to deceive others, and to tell them that they want many more to go over the fea, and be as they are. So in that refpect, wherein it may be faid that they will fell one another, they are only enfnared and enlifted to be fervants, kept like fome of thofe which they fee at the factories, which, for fome gewgaws, as prefents given to themfelves and friends, they are thereby enticed to go; and fomething after the fame manner that Eaft-India foldiers are procured in Britain; and the inhabitants here, juft as much fell themfelves, and one another, as they do; and the kid-nappers here, and the flave-procurers in Africa, are much alike. But many other barbarous methods are made ufe of by the vile inftigators, procurers and enfnarers of men; and fome of the wicked and profligate princes and chiefs of Africa accept of prefents, from the Europeans, to procure a certain number of flaves; and thereby they are wickedly inftigated to go to war with one another on purpofe to get them, which produces many terrible depredations; and fometimes when thofe engagements are entered into, and they find themfelves defeated of their purpofe, it has happened that fome of their own people have fallen a facrifice to their avarice and cruelty. And it may be faid of the Europeans, that they have made ufe of every infidious method to procure flaves whenever they can, and in whatever manner they can lay hold of them, and that their forts and factories are the avowed dens of thieves for robbers, plunderers and depredators.

But again, as to the Africans felling their own wives and children, nothing can be more oppofite to every thing they hold dear and valuable;

and

and nothing can diftrefs them more, than to part with any of their relations and friends. Such are the tender feelings of parents for their children, that, for the lofs of a child, they feldom can be rendered happy, even with the intercourfe and enjoyment of their friends, for years. For any man to think that it fhould be otherwife when he may fee a thoufand inftances of a natural inftinct, even in the brute creation, where they have a fympathetic feeling for their offspring; it muft be great want of confideration not to think, that much more than meerly what is natural to animals, fhould in a higher degree be implanted in the breaft of every part of the rational creation of man. And what man of feeling can help lamenting the lofs of parents, friends, liberty, and perhaps property and other valuable and dear connections. Thofe people annually brought away from Guinea, are born as free, and are brought up with as great a predilection for their own country, freedom and liberty, as the fons and daughters of fair Britain. Their free fubjects are trained up to a kind of military fervice, not fo much by the defire of the chief, as by their own voluntary inclination. It is looked upon as the greateft refpect they can fhew to their king, to ftand up for his and their own defence in time of need. Their different chieftains, which bear a reliance on the great chief, or king, exercife a kind of government fomething like that feudal inftitution which prevailed fome time in Scotland. In this refpect, though the common people are free, they often fuffer by the villainy of their different chieftains, and by the wars and feuds which happen among them. Neverthelefs their freedom and rights are as dear to them, as thofe

privileges

privileges are to other people. And it may be faid that freedom, and the liberty of enjoying their own privileges, burns with as much zeal and fervour in the breaft of an Æthiopian, as in the breaft of any inhabitant on the globe.

But the fupporters and favourers of flavery make other things a pretence and an excufe in their own defence; fuch as, that they find that it was admitted under the Divine inftitution by Mofes, as well as the long continued practice of different nations for ages; and that the Africans are peculiarly marked out by fome fignal prediction in nature and complexion for that purpofe.

This feems to be the greateft bulwark of defence which the advocates and favourers of flavery can advance, and what is generally talked of in their favour by thofe who do not underftand it. I fhall confider it in that view, whereby it will appear, that they deceive themfelves and miflead others. Men are never more liable to be drawn into error, than when truth is made ufe of in a guileful manner to feduce them. Thofe who do not believe the fcriptures to be a Divine revelation, cannot, confiftently with themfelves, make the law of Mofes, or any mark or prediction they can find refpecting any particular fet of men, as found in the facred writings, any reafon that one clafs of men fhould enflave another. In that refpect, all that they have to enquire into fhould be, whether it be right, or wrong, that any part of the human fpecies fhould enflave another; and when that is the cafe, the Africans, though not fo learned, are juft as wife as the Europeans; and when the matter is left to human wifdom, they are both liable to err. But what the light of nature, and the dictates of reafon,
when

when rightly confidered, teach, is, that no man
ought to enflave another; and fome, who have
been rightly guided thereby, have made noble
defences for the univerfal natural rights and privileges of all men. But in this cafe, when the
learned take neither revelation nor reafon for
their guide, they fall into as great, and worfe errors, than the unlearned; for they only make
ufe of that fyftem of Divine wifdom, which
fhould guide them into truth, when they can
find or pick out any thing that will fuit their
purpofe, or that they can pervert to fuch—the
very means of leading themfelves and others into
error. And, in confequence thereof, the pretences that fome men make ufe of for holding of
flaves, muft be evidently the groffeft perverfion
of reafon, as well as an inconfiftent and diabolical ufe of the facred writings. For it muft be a
ftrange perverfion of reafon, and a wrong ufe or
difbelief of the facred writings, when any thing
found there is fo perverted by them, and fet up
as a precedent and rule for men to commit wickednefs. They had better have no reafon, and no
belief in the fcriptures, and make no ufe of them
at all, than only to believe, and make ufe of that
which leads them into the moft abominable evil
and wickednefs of dealing unjuftly with their fellow men.

But this will appear evident to all men that believe the fcriptures, that every reafon neceffary is
given that they fhould be believed; and, in this
cafe, that they afford us this information : " That
" all mankind did fpring from one original, and
" that there are no different fpecies among men.
" For God who made the world, hath made of
" one blood all the nations of men that dwell on
" all

" all the face of the earth." Wherefore we may juftly infer, as there are no inferior fpecies, but all of one blood and of one nature, that there does not an inferiority fubfift, or depend, on their colour, features or form, whereby fome men make a pretence to enflave others; and confequently, as they have all one creator, one original, made of one blood, and all brethren defcended from one father, it never could be lawful and juft for any nation, or people, to opprefs and enflave another.

And again, as all the prefent inhabitants of the world fprang from the family of Noah, and were then all of one complexion, there is no doubt, but the difference which we now find, took its rife very rapidly after they became difperfed and fettled on the different parts of the globe. There feems to be a tendency to this, in many inftances, among children of the fame parents, having different colour of hair and features from one another. And God alone who eftablifhed the courfe of nature, can bring about and eftablifh what variety he pleafes; and it is not in the power of man to make one hair white or black. But among the variety which it hath pleafed God to eftablifh and caufed to take place, we may meet with fome analogy in nature, that as the bodies of men are tempered with a different degree to enable them to endure the refpective climates of their habitations, fo their colours vary, in fome degree, in a regular gradation from the equator towards either of the poles. However, there are other incidental caufes arifing from time and place, which conftitute the moft diftinguifhing variety of colour, form, appearance and features, as peculiar to the inhabitants of one tract of country,

country, and differing in fomething from thofe
in another, even in the fame latitudes, as well as
from thofe in different climates. Long cuftom
and the different way of living among the feveral
inhabitants of the different parts of the earth, has
a very great effect in diftinguifhing them by a
difference of features and complexion. Thefe
effects are eafy to be feen ; as to the caufes, it is
fufficient for us to know, that all is the work of
an Almighty hand. Therefore, as we find the
diftribution of the human fpecies inhabiting the
barren, as well as the moft fruitful parts of the
earth, and the cold as well as the moft hot, differing from one another in complexion according to their fituation ; it may be reafonably, as
well as religioufly, inferred, that He who placed
them in their various fituations, hath extended
equally his care and protection to all ; and from
thence, that it becometh unlawful to counteract
his benignity, by reducing others of different
complexions to undeferved bondage.

According, as we find that the difference of
colour among men is only incidental, and equally natural to all, and agreeable to the place of
their habitation ; and that if nothing elfe be different or contrary among them, but that of features and complexion, in that refpect, they are
all equally alike entitled to the enjoyment of every mercy and bleffing of God. But there are
fome men of that complexion, becaufe they are
not black, whofe ignorance and infolence leads
them to think, that thofe who are black, were
marked out in that manner by fome fignal interdiction or curfe, as originally defcending from
their progenitors. To thofe I muft fay, that the
only mark which we read of, as generally alluded

to,

to, and by them applied wrongfully, is that mark or fign which God gave to Cain, to affure him that he fhould not be deftroyed. Cain underftood by the nature of the crime he had committed, that the law required death, or cutting off, as the punifhment thereof. But God in his providence doth not always punifh the wicked in this life according to their enormous crimes, (we are told, by a facred poet, that he faw the wicked flourifhing like a green bay tree) though he generally marks them out by fome fignal token of his vengeance; and that is a fure token of it, when men become long hardened in their wickednefs. The denunciation that paffed upon Cain was, that he fhould be a fugitive and a vagabond on the earth, bearing the curfe and reproach of his iniquity; and the reft of men were prohibited as much from meddling with him, or defiling their hands by him, as it naturally is, not to pull down the dead carcafe of an atrocious criminal, hung up in chains by the laws of his country. But allow the mark fet upon Cain to have confifted in a black fkin, ftill no conclufion can be drawn at all, that any of the black people are of that defcent, as the whole pofterity of Cain were deftroyed in the univerfal deluge.

Only Noah, a righteous and juft man, who found grace in the fight of God, and his three fons, Japheth, Shem and Ham, and their wives, eight perfons, were preferved from the univerfal deluge, in the ark which Noah was directed to build. The three fons of Noah had each children born after the flood, from whom all the prefent world of men defcended. But it came to pafs, in the days of Noah, that an interdiction, or curfe, took place in the family of Ham, and that the

D   defcendants

defcendants of one of his fons fhould become the fervants of fervants to their brethren, the defcendants of Shem and Japheth. This affords a grand pretence for the fapporters of the African flavery to build a falfe notion upon, as it is found by hiftory that Africa, in general, was peopled by the defcendants of Ham; but thev forget, that the prediction has already been fulfilled as far as it can go.

There can be no doubt, that there was a fhameful mifconduct in Ham himfelf, by what is related of him; but the fault, according to the prediction and curfe, defcended onlv to the families of the defcendants of his youngeft fon, Canaan. The occafion was, that Noah, his father, had drank wine, and (perhaps unawares) became inebriated by it, and fell afleep in his tent. It feems that Ham was greatly deficient of that filial virtue as either becoming a father or a fon, went into his father's tent, and, it may be fuppofed, in an undecent manner, he had fuffered his own fon, Canaan, fo to meddle with, or uncover, his father, that he faw his nakednefs; for which he did not check the audacious rudenefs of Canaan, but went and told his brethren without in ridicule of his aged parent. This rude audacious behaviour of Canaan, and the obloquy of his father Ham, brought on him the curfe of his grandfather, Noah, but he bleffed Shem and Japheth for their decent and filial virtues, and denounced, in the fpirit of prophecy, that Canaan fhould be their fervant, and fhould ferve them.

It may be obferved, that it is a great misfortune for children, when their parents are not endowed with that wifdom and prudence which is neceffary for the early initiation of their offspring

in

in the paths of virtue and righteoufnefs. Ham was guilty of the offence as well as his fon; he did not pity the weaknefs of his father, who was overcome with wine in that day wherein, it is likely, he had fome folemn work to do. But the prediction and curfe refted wholly upon the off-fpring of Canaan, who fettled in the land known by his name, in the weft of Afia, as is evident from the facred writings. The Canaanites became an exceeding wicked people, and were vifited with many calamities, according to the prediction of Noah, for their abominable wickednefs and idolatry.

Chederluomer, a defcendant of Shem, reduced the Canaanitifh kingdoms to a tributary fubjection; and fome time after, upon their revolt, invaded and pillaged their country. Not long after Sodom, Gomorrah, Admah and Zeboim, four kingdoms of the Canaanites were overthrown for their great wickednefs, and utterly deftroyed by fire and brimftone from heaven. The Hebrews, chiefly under Mofes, Jofhua and Barak, as they were directed by God, cut off moft of the other Canaanitifh kingdoms, and reduced many of them to fubjection and vaffalage. Thofe who fettled in the north-weft of Canaan, and formed the once flourifhing ftates of Tyre and Sidon, were by the Affyrians, the Chaldeans, and the Perfians fuccef-fively reduced to great mifery and bondage; but chiefly by the Greeks, the Romans, and the Sa-racens, and laftly by the Turks, they were com-pleatly and totally ruined, and have no more fince been a diftinct people among the different nations. Many of the Canaanites who fled away in the Time of Jofhua, became mingled with the different nations, and fome hiftorians think that

fome

some of them came to England, and settled about Cornwall, as far back as that time; so that, for any thing that can be known to the contrary, there may be some of the descendants of that wicked generation still subsisting among the slave holders in the West-Indies. For if the curse of God ever rested upon them, or upon any other men, the only visible mark thereof was always upon those who committed the most outrageous acts of violence and oppression. But colour and complexion has nothing to do with that mark; every wicked man, and the enslavers of others, bear the stamp of their own iniquity, and that mark which was set upon Cain.

Now, the descendants of the other three sons of Ham, were not included under the curse of his father, and as they dispersed and settled on the different parts of the earth, they became also sundry distinct and very formidable nations. Cush, the oldest, settled in the south-west of Arabia, and his descendants were anciently known to the Hebrews by the name of Cushites, or Cushie; one of his sons, Nimrod, founded the kingdom of Babylon, in Asia; and the others made their descent southward, by the Red Sea, and came over to Abyssinia and Ethiopia, and, likely, dispersed themselves throughout all the southern and interior parts of Africa; and as they lived mostly under the torrid zone, or near the tropics, they became black, as being natural to the inhabitants of those sultry hot climates; and, in that case, their complexion bears the signification of the name of their original progenitor, Cush, as known by the Hebrews by that name, both on the east and on the west, beyond the Red Sea; but the Greeks called them Ethiopians, or black faced people.

people. The Egyptians and Philiftines were the defcendants of Mizraim, and the country which they inhabited was called the land of Mizraim, and Africa, in general, was anciently called the whole land of Ham. Phut, another of his fons, alfo fettled on the weft of Egypt, and as the youngeft were obliged to emigrate fartheft, afterwards difperfed themfelves chiefly up the fouth of the Mediterranean fea, towards Lybia and Mauritania, and might early mingle with fome of the Cufhites on the more fouthern, and, chiefly, on the weftern parts of Africa. But all thefe might be followed by fome other families and tribes from Afia; and fome think that Africa got its name from the King of Lybia marrying a daughter of Aphra, one of the defcendants of Abraham, by Keturah.

But it may be reafonably fuppofed, that the moft part of the black people in Africa, are the defcendants of the Cufhites, towards the eaft, the fouth, and interior parts, and chiefly of the Phutians towards the weft; and the various revolutions and changes which have happened among them have rather been local than univerfal; fo that whoever their original progenitors were, as defcending from one generation to another, in a long continuance, it becomes natural for the inhabitants of that tract of country to be a dark black, in general. The learned and thinking part of men, who can refer to hiftory, muft know, that nothing with refpect to colour, nor any mark or curfe from any original prediction, can in anywife be more particularly afcribed to the Africans than to any other people of the human fpecies, fo as to afford any pretence why they fhould be more evil treated, perfecuted and enflaved, than

D 3   any

any other. Nothing but ignorance, and the dreams of a viciated imagination, arifing from the general countenance given to the evil practice of wicked men, to ftrengthen their hands in wickednefs, could ever make any perfon to fancy otherwife, or ever to think that the ftealing, kidnapping, enflaving, perfecuting or killing a black man, is in any way and manner lefs criminal, than the fame evil treatment of any other man of another complexion.

But again, in anfwer to another part of the pretence which the favourers of flavery make ufe of in their defence, that flavery was an ancient cuftom, and that it became the prevalent and univerfal practice of many different barbarous nations for ages: This muft be granted; but not becaufe it was right, or any thing like right and equity. A lawful fervitude was always neceffary, and became contingent with the very nature of human fociety. But when the laws of civilization were broken through, and when the rights and properties of others were invaded, that brought the oppreffed into a kind of compulfive fervitude, though often not compelled to it by thofe whom they were obliged to feive. This arofe from the different depredations and robberies which were committed upon one another; the helplefs were obliged to feek protection from fuch as could fupport them, and to give unto them their fervice, in order to preferve themfelves from want, and to deliver them from the injury either of men or beafts. For while civil fociety continued in a rude ftate, even among the eftablifhers of kingdoms, when they became powerful and proud, as they wanted to enlarge their territories, they drove and expelled others from
their

their peaceable habitations, who were not fo
powerful as themfelves. This made thofe who
were robbed of their fubftance, and drove from
the place of their abode, make their efcape to
fuch as could and would help them; but when
fuch a relief could not be found, they were obliged to fubmit to the yoke of their oppreffors, who,
in many cafes, would not yield them any protection upon any terms. Wherefore, when their
lives were in danger otherwife, and they could
not find any help, they were obliged to fell themfelves for bond fervants to fuch as would buy
them, when they could not get a fervice that was
better. But as foon as buyers could be found,
robbers began their traffic to enfnare others, and
fuch as fell into their hands were carried captive
by them, and were obliged to fubmit to their being fold by them into the hands of other robbers,
for there are few buyers of men, who intend thereby to make them free, and fuch as they buy are
generally fubjected to hard labour and bondage.
Therefore at all times, while a man is a flave, he
is ftill in captivity, and under the jurifdiction of
robbers; and every man who keeps a flave, is a
robber, whenever he compels him to his fervice
without giving him a juft reward. The barely
fupplying his flave with fome neceffary things, to
keep him in life, is no reward at all, that is only
for his own fake and benefit; and the very nature
of compulfion and taking away the liberty of
others, as well as their property, is robbery; and
that kind of fervice which fubjects men to a ftate
of flavery, muft at all times, and in every cir-
cumftance, be a barbarous, inhuman and unjuft
dealing with our fellow men. A voluntary fervice, and flavery, are quite different things; but
in

in ancient times, in whatever degree flavery was admitted, and whatever hardfhips they were, in general, fubjected to, it was not nearly fo bad as the modern barbarous and cruel Weft-India flavery.

Now, in refpect to that kind of fervitude which was admitted into the law of Mofes, that was not contrary to the natural liberties of men, but a ftate of equity and juftice, according as the nature and circumftances of the times required. There was no more harm in entering into a covenant with another man as a bond-fervant, than there is for two men to enter into partnerfhip the one with the other; and fometimes the nature of the cafe may be, and their bufinefs require it, that the one may find money and live at a diftance and eafe, and the other manage the bufinefs for him: So a bond-fervant was generally the fteward in a man's houfe, and fometimes his heir. There was no harm in buying a man who was in a ftate of captivity and bondage by others, and keeping him in fervitude till fuch time as his purchafe was redeemed by his labour and fervice. And there could be no harm in paying a man's debts, and keeping him in fervitude until fuch time as an equitable agreement of compofition was paid by him. And fo, in general, whether they had been bought or fold in order to pay their juft debts when they became poor, or were bought from fuch as held them in an unlawful captivity, the ftate of bondage which they and their children fell under, among the Ifraelites, was into that of a vaffalage ftate, which rather might be termed a deliverance from debt and captivity, than a ftate of flavery. In that vaffalage ftate which they were reduced to, they had a tax of fome fervice to

pay,

pay, which might only be reckoned equivalent to a poor man in England paying rent for his cottage. In this fair land of liberty, there are many thousands of the inhabitants who have no right to so much land as an inch of ground to set their foot upon, so as to take up their residence upon it, without paying a lawful and reasonable vassalage of rent for it—and yet the whole community is free from slavery. And so, likewise, those who were reduced to a state of servitude, or vassalage, in the land of Israel, were not negociable like chattels and goods; nor could they be disposed of like cattle and beasts of burden, or ever transferred or disposed of without their own consent; and perhaps not one man in all the land of Israel would buy another man, unless that man was willing to serve him. And when any man had gotten such a servant, as he had entered into a covenant of agreement with, as a bond-servant, if the man liked his master and his service, he could not oblige him to go away; and it sometimes happened, that they refused to go out free when the year of jubilee came. But even that state of servitude which the Canaanites were reduced to, among those who survived the general overthrow of their country, was nothing worse, in many respects, than that of poor labouring people in any free country. Their being made hewers of wood and drawers of water, were laborious employments; but they were paid for it in such a manner as the nature of their service required, and were supplied with abundance of such necessaries of life as they and their families had need of; and they were at liberty, if they chose, to go away, there was no restriction laid on them. They were not hunted after, and a reward offered for their heads,

heads, as it is the cafe in the Weft-Indies for any that can find a ftrayed flave; and he who can bring fuch a head warm reeking with his blood, as a token that he had murdered him—inhuman and fhocking to think!—he is paid for it; and, cruel and dreadful as it is, that law is ftill in force in fome of the Britifh colonies.

But the Canaanites, although they were predicted to be reduced to a ftate of fervitude, and bondage to that poor and menial employment, fared better than the Weft-India flaves; for when they were brought into that ftate of fervitude, they were often employed in an honourable fervice. The Nethenims, and others, were to affift in the facred folemnities and worfhip of God at the Temple of Jerufalem. They had the fame laws and immunities refpecting the folemn days and fabbaths, as their mafters the Ifraelites, and they were to keep and obferve them. But they were not fuffered, much lefs required, to labour in their own fpots of ufeful ground on the days of facred reft from worldly employment; and that, if they did not improve the culture of it, in thefe times and feafons, they might otherwife perifh for hunger and want; as it is the cafe of the Weft-India flaves, by their inhuman, infidel, hardhearted mafters. And, therefore, this may be juftly faid, that whatever fervitude that was, or by whatever name it may be called, that the fervice which was required by the people of Ifrael in old time, was of a far milder nature, than that which became the prevalent practice of other different and barbarous nations; and, if compared with modern flavery, it might be called liberty, equity, and felicity, in refpect to that abominable, mean, beaftly, cruel, bloody flavery carried

on

on by the inhuman, barbarous Europeans, againſt the poor unfortunate Black Africans.

But again, this may be averred, that the ſervitude which took place under the ſanction of the divine law, in the time of Moſes, and what was enjoined as the civil and religious polity of the people of Iſrael, was in nothing contrary to the natural rights and common liberties of men, though it had an appearance as ſuch for great and wiſe ends. The Divine Law Giver, in his good providence, for great and wiſe purpoſes intended by it, has always admitted into the world riches and poverty, proſperity and adverſity, high and low, rich and poor; and in ſuch manner, as in all their variety and difference, mutation and change, there is nothing ſet forth in the written law, by Moſes, contrary, unbecoming, or inconſiſtent with that goodneſs of himſelf, as the wiſe and righteous Governor of the Univerſe. Thoſe things admitted into the law, that had a ſeeming appearance contrary to the natural liberties of men, were only ſo admitted for a local time, to point out, and to eſtabliſh, and to give inſtruction thereby, in an analogous alluſion to other things.

And therefore, ſo far as I have been able to conſult the law written by Moſes, concerning that kind of ſervitude admitted by it, I can find nothing imported thereby, in the leaſt degree, to warrant the modern practice of ſlavery. But, on the contrary, and what was principally intended thereby, and in the moſt particular manner, as reſpecting Chriſtians, that it contains the ſtrongeſt prohibition againſt it. And every Chriſtian man, that can read his Bible, may find that which is of the greateſt importance for himſelf to know, implied even under the very inſtitution of bond-ſervants ;

vants; and that the ftate of bondage which the law denounces and defcribes, was thereby fo intended to point out fomething neceffary, as well as fimilar to all the other ritual and ceremonial fervices; and that the whole is fet forth in fuch a manner, as containing the very effence and foundation of the Chriftian religion. And, moreover, that it muft appear evident to any Chriftian believer, that it was neceffary that all thefe things fhould take place, and as the moft beautiful fabric of Divine goodnefs, that in all their variety, and in all their forms, they fhould ftand recorded under the fanction of the Divine law.

And this muft be obferved, that it hath fo pleafed the Almighty Creator, to eftablifh all the variety of things in nature, different complexions and other circumftances among men, and to record the various tranfactions of his own providence, with all the ceremonial œconomy written in the books of Mofes, as more particularly refpecting and enjoined to the Ifraelitifh nation and people, for the ufe of facred language, in order to convey wifdom to the fallen apoftate human race. Wherefore, all the various things eftablifhed, admitted and recorded, whether natural, moral, typical or ceremonial, with all the various things in nature referred to, were fo ordered and admitted, as figures, types and emblems, and other fymbolical reprefentations, to bring forward, ufher in, hold forth and illuftrate that moft amazing tranfaction, and the things concerning it, of all things the moft wonderful that ever could take place amongft the univerfe of intelligent beings; as in that, and the things concerning it, of the falvation of apoftate men, and the wonderful benignity of their Almighty Redeemer.

Whoever

Whoever will give a ſerious and unprejudiced attention to the various things alluded to in the language of ſacred writ, muſt ſee reaſon to believe that they imply a purpoſe and deſign far more glorious and important, than what ſeems generally to be underſtood by them; and to point to objeꞔts and events far more extenſive and intereſting, than what is generally aſcribed to them. But as the grand eligibility and importance of thoſe things, implied and pointed out in ſacred writ, and the right underſtanding thereof, belongs to the ſublime ſcience of metaphyſics and theology to enforce, illuſtrate and explain, I ſhall only ſeleꞔt a few inſtances, which I think have a relation to my ſubjeꞔt in hand.

Among other things it may be conſidered, that the different colours and complexions among men were intended for another purpoſe and deſign, than that of being only eligible in the variety of the ſcale of nature. And, accordingly, had it been otherwiſe, and if there had never been any black people among the children of men, nor any ſpotted leopards among the beaſts of the earth, ſuch an inſtruꞔtive queſtion, by the prophet, could not have been propoſed, as this, *Can the Ethiopian change his ſkin, or the leopard his ſpots? Then, may ye alſo do good, that are accuſtomed to do evil.* Jer. xiii. 23. The inſtruꞔtion intended by this is evident, that it was a convincing and forcible argument to ſhew, that none among the fallen and apoſtate race of men, can by any effort of their own, change their nature from the blackneſs and guilt of the ſable dye of ſin and polution, or alter their way accuſtomed to do evil, from the variegated ſpots of their iniquity; and that ſuch a change is as impoſſible to be totally and radically
effeꞔted

effected by them, as it is for a black man to change the colour of his skin, or the leopard to alter his spots. But these differences of a natural variety amongst the things themselves, is in every respect equally innocent, and what they cannot alter or change, was made to be so, and in the most eligible and primary design, were so intended for the very purposes of instructive language to men. And by these extreme differences of colour, it was intended to point out and shew to the white man, that there is a sinful blackness in his own nature, which he can no more change, than the external blackness which he sees in another can be rendered otherwise; and it likewise holds out to the black man, that the sinful blackness of his own nature is such, that he can no more alter, than the outward appearance of his colour can be brought to that of another. And this is imported by it, that there is an inherent evil in every man, contrary to that which is good; and that all men are like Ethiopians (even God's elect) in a state of nature and unregeneracy, they are black with original sin, and spotted with actual transgression, which they cannot reverse. But to this truth, asserted of blackness, I must add another glorious one. All thanks and eternal praise be to God! His infinite wisdom and goodness has found out a way of renovation, and has opened a fountain through the blood of Jesus, for sin and for uncleanness, wherein all the stains and blackest dyes of sin and polution can be washed away for ever, and the darkest sinner be made to shine as the brightest angel in heaven. And for that end and purpose, God alone has appointed all the channels of conveyance of the everlasting Gospel for these healing and purifying streams of the

water

water of life to run in, and to bring life and sal-
vation, with light and gladnefs to men; but he
denounces woe to thofe who do not receive it
themfelves, but hinder and debar others who
would, from coming to thofe falutary ftreams for
life : Yet not alone confined to thefe, nor hindered in his purpofe by any oppofers, He, who can
open the eyes of the blind, and make the deaf to
hear, can open ftreams in the defart, and make
his benignity to flow, and his falvation to vifit,
even the meaneft and moft ignorant man, in the
darkeft fhades of nature, as well as the moft
learned on the earth; and he ufually carries on his
own gracious work of quickening and redeeming
grace, in a fecret, fovereign manner. To this I
muft again obferve, and what I chiefly intended
by this fimilitude, that the external blacknefs of
the Ethiopians, is as innocent and natural, as
fpots in the leopards; and that the difference of
colour and complexion, which in hath pleafed
God to appoint among men, are no more unbecoming unto either of them, than the different
fhades of the rainbow are unfeemly to the whole,
or unbecoming to any part of that apparent arch.
It does not alter the nature and quality of a man,
whether he wears a black or a white coat, whether
he puts it on or ftrips it off, he is ftill the fame
man. And fo likewife, when a man comes to
die, it makes no difference whether he was black
or white, whether he was male or female, whether he was great or fmall, or whether he was old
or young; none of thefe differences alter the ef-
fentiality of the man, any more than he had wore
a black or a white coat and thrown it off for ever.
    Another form of inftruction for the fame pur-
pofe, may be taken from the flavery and oppref-
                                              fion

fion which men have committed upon one another, as well as that kind of bondage and fervitude which was admitted under the fanction of
the Divine law. But there is nothing fet forth
in the law as a rule, or any thing recorded therein that can ftand as a precedent, or make it lawful, for men to practice flavery; nor can any laws
in favour of flavery be deduced from thence, for
to enflave men, be otherwife, than as unwarrantble,
as it would be unneceffary and wrong, to order
and command the facrifices of beafts to be ftill
continued   Now the great thing imported by it,
and what is chiefly to be deduced from it in this
refpect, is, that fo far as the law concerning bond-
fervants, and that eftablifhment of fervitude, as admitted in the Mofaical inftitution, was fet forth,
it was thereby intended to prefigure and point
out, that fpiritual fubjection and bondage to fin,
that all mankind, by their original transgreffion,
were fallen into.   All men in their fallen depraved ftate, being under a fpirit of bondage, funk
into a nature of brutifh carnality, and by the lufts
thereof, they are carried captive and enflaved;
and the confequence is, that they are fold under
fin and in bondage to iniquity, and carried captive by the devil at his will.   This being the cafe,
the thing proves itfelf; for if there had been no
evil and fin amongft men, there never would have
been any kind of bondage, flavery and oppreffion
found amongft them; and if there was none of
thefe things to be found, the great caufe of it
could not, in the prefent fituation of men, be
pointed out to them in that eligible manner as it
is.   Wherefore it was neceffary that fomething
of that bondage and fervitude fhould be admitted
into the ritual law for a figurative ufe, which, in
                                          all

all other refpects and circumftances, was, in itfelf, contrary to the whole tenure of the law, and
naturally in itfelf unlawful for men to practice.

Nothing but heavenly wifdom, and heavenly
grace, can teach men to underftand. The moft
deplorable of all things is, that the dreadful fituation of our univerfalde praved ftate, which all
mankind lyeth under, is fuch, that thofe who are
not redeemed in time, muft for ever continue to
be the fubjects of eternal bondage and mifery.
Bleffed be God! he hath appointed and fet up a
deliverance; and the Saviour of Men is an Almighty Redeemer. When God, the Almighty
Redeemer and Saviour of his people, brought his
Ifrael out of Egypt and temporal bondage, it was
intended and defigned thereby, to fet up an emblematical reprefentation of their deliverance from
the power and captivity of fin, and from the dominion of that evil and malignant fpirit, who had
with exquifite fubtilty and guile at firft feduced
the original progenitors of mankind. And when
they were brought to the promifed land, and had
gotten deliverance, and fubdued their enemies
under them, they were to reign over them ; and
their laws refpecting bond-fervants, and other
things of that nature, were to denote, that they
were to keep under and in fubjection the whole
body of their evil affections and lufts. This is fo
declared by the Apoftle, that the law is fpiritual,
and intended for fpiritual ufes. The general'ftate
of flavery which took place in the world, among
other enormous crimes of wicked men might have
ferved for an emblem and fimilitude of our fpiritual bondage and flavery to fin; but, unlefs it
had been admitted into the fpiritual and divine
law, it could not have ftood and become an em-

E　　　　　　　　blem

blem that there was any fpiritual reftoration and
deliverance afforded to us. By that which is
evil in captivity and flavery among men, we are
thereby fo reprefented to be under a like fubjection to fin; but by what is inftituted in the law
by Mofes, in that refpect we are thereby reprefented as Ifrael to have dominion over fin, and to
rule over and keep in fubjection all our fpiritual
enemies. And, therefore, any thing which had
a feeming appearance in favour of flavery, fo far
as it was admitted into the law, was to fhew that
it was not natural and innocent, like that of different colours among men, but as neceffary to be
made an emblem of what was intended by it,
and, confequently, as it ftands enjoined among
other typical reprefentations, was to fhew that
every thing of any evil appearance of it, was to
be removed; and to end with the other typical
and ceremonial injunctions, when the time of
that difpenfation was over. This muft appear
evident to all Chriftian believers; and fince therefore all thefe things are fulfilled in the eftablifhment of Chriftianity, there is now nothing re-
maining in the law for a rule of practice to men,
but the ever abiding obligations, and ever binding injunctions of moral rectitude, juftice, equity and righteoufnefs. All the other things in the
Divine law, are for fpiritual ufes and fimilitudes,
for giving inftruction to the wife, and underftanding to the upright in heart, that the man of
God may be perfect, throughly furnifhed unto all
good works.

Among other things alfo, the wars of the Ifraelites, and the extirpation of the Canaanites,
and other circumftances as recorded in facred
hiftory, were intended to give inftruction to men,
but

but have often been perverted to the moſt flagrant abuſe, and even inverted to the moſt notorious purpoſes, for men to embolden themſelves to commit wickedneſs. Every poſſeſſion that men enjoy upon earth are the gifts of God, and he who gives them, may either take them away again from men, or he may take men away themſelves from the earth, as it pleaſeth him. But who dare, even with Lucifer, the malignant devourer of the world, think to imitate the moſt High ? The extirpation of the Canaanites out of their land, was ſo ordered, not only to puniſh them for their idolatry and abominable wickedneſs, but alſo to ſhew forth the honour of his power, and the ſovereignty of him who is the only potent one that reigneth over the nations ; that all men at that time might learn to fear and know him who is Jehovah ; and ever ſince that it might continue a ſtanding memorial of him, and a ſtandard of honor unto him who doth according to his will among the armies of heaven, and whatever pleaſeth him with the inhabitants of the earth. And, in general, theſe tranſactions ſtand recorded for an emblematical uſe and ſimilitude, in the ſpiritual warfare of every true Iſraelite throughout all the ages of time. Every real believer and valiant champion in the knowledge and faith of their Omnipotent Saviour and Almighty Deliverer, as the very nature of Chriſtianity requires and enjoins, knoweth the uſe of theſe things, *and they know how to endure hardneſs as good ſoldiers of Jeſus Chriſt.* They have many battles to fight with their unbelief, the perverſeneſs of their nature, evil tempers and beſetting ſins, theſe Canaanites which ſtill dwell in their land. They are ſo ſurrounded with adverſaries, that

E 2   they

they have need always to be upon their guard, and to have all their armour on. They are *commanded to caſt off the works of darkneſs, and to put on the whole armour of righteouſneſs and light ; and that they may be ſtrong in the Lord, and in the power of his might.* For it is required *that they ſhould be able to ſtand againſt the wiles of the devil, the powers of the rulers of the darkneſs of this world, againſt ſpiritual wickedneſs in high places.* And as their foes are *mighty and tall like the Anakims, and fenced up to heaven,* they muſt be mighty warriors, *men of renown, valiant for the truth, ſtrong in the faith, fighting the Lord's battles, and overcoming all their enemies, through the dear might of the Great Captain of their ſalvation.* In this warfare, ſhould they meet with ſome mighty *Agag,* ſome ſtrong corruption, or beſetting ſin, they are commanded *to cut it down,* and with the ſword of Samuel *to hew it to pieces before the Lord.* This, in its literal ſenſe, may ſeem harſh, as if Samuel had been cruel; and ſo will our ſins, and other ſinners inſinuate, and tell us not to mind ſuch things as the perfect law of God requires. But if we conſider that the Lord God who breathed into man the breath of life, can ſuſpend and take it away when he pleaſeth, and that there is not a moment we have to exiſt, wherein that life may not be ſuſpended before the next : it was therefore of an indifferent matter for that man Agag, when the Lord, who hath the breath and life of every man in his hand, had appointed him at that time to die, for his great wickedneſs and the murders committed by him, whether he was ſlain by Samuel or any other means. But what Samuel, the ſervant of the Lord, did in that inſtance, was in obedience to his voice, and in itſelf

felf a righteous deed, and a juft judgment upon Agag. And the matter imported by it, was alfo intended to fhew, that all our Amalekite fins, and even the chief and darling of them, the avaricious and covetous Agags, fhould be cut off for ever. But if we fpare them, and leave them to remain alive in ftubborn difobedience to the law and commandments of God, we fhould in that cafe, be like Saul, cut off ourfelves from the kingdom of his grace. According to this view, it may fuffice to fhew (and what infinite wifdom intended, no doubt,) that a wife and righteous ufe may be made of thofe very things, which otherwife are generally perverted to wrong purpofes.

And now, as to thefe few inftances which I have collected from that facred hypothefis, whereby it is fhewn, that other things are implied and to be underftood by the various incidents as recorded in facred writ, with a variety of other things in nature, bearing an analogous allufion to things of the greateft importance for every Chriftian man to know and underftand; and that the whole of the ritual law, though thefe things themfelves are not to be again repeated, is of that nature and ufe as never to be forgot. And therefore to fuppofe, or for any Chriftians to fay, that they have nothing to do with thofe things now in the right ufe thereof, and what was intended and imported thereby refpecting themfelves, would be equally as abfurd as to hear them fpeaking in the language of devils; and they might as well fay as they did, when fpeaking out of the demoniac, that they have nothing to do with Chrift.

Having thus endeavoured to fhew, and what, I think, muft appear evident and obvious, that

E 3 none

none of all thefe grand pretenfions, as generally
made ufe of by the favourers of flavery. to encourage and embolden them, in that iniquitous
traffic, can have any foundation or fhadow of
truth to fupport them; and that there is nothing
in nature, reafon, and fcripture can be found,
in any manner or way, to warrant the enflaving
of black people more than others.

But I am aware that fome of thefe arguments
will weigh nothing againft fuch men as do not
believe the fcriptures themfelves, nor care to underftand; but let them be aware not to make ufe
of thefe things againft us which they do not believe, or whatever pretence they may have for
committing violence againft us. Any property
taken away from others, whether by ftealth,
fraud, or violence, muft be wrong; but to take
away men themfelves, and keep them in flavery,
muft be worfe. *Skin for fkin, all that a man hath
would he give for his life*; and would rather lofe
his property to any amount whatever, than to
have his liberty taken away, and be kept as a
flave. It muft be an inconceivable fallacy to
think otherwife: none but the inconfiderate,
moft obdurate and ftubborn, could ever think
that it was right to enflave others. *But the way
of the wicked is brutifh: his own iniquity fhall
take the wicked himfelf, and he fhall be holden with
the cords of his fins: he fhall die without inftruction,
and in the greatnefs of his folly he fhall go aftray.*

Among the various fpecies of men that commit rapine, and violence, and murders, and theft,
upon their fellow-creatures, like the ravenous
beafts of the night, prowling for their prey, there
are alfo thofe that fet out their heads in the open
day, oppofing all the obligations of civilization
among

among men, and breaking through all the laws of juftice and equity to them, and making even the very things which are analogous to the obligations, which ought to warn and prohibit them, a pretence for their iniquity and injuftice. Such are the infidious merchants and pirates that gladen their oars with the carnage and captivity of men, and the vile negociators and enflavers of the human fpecies. The prohibitions againft them are fo ftrong, that, in order to break through and to commit the moft notorious and flagrant crimes with impunity, they are obliged to oil their poifonous pretences with various perverfions of fundrv tranfactions of things even in facred writ, that the acrimonious points of their arfenic may be fwallowed down the better, and the evil effects of their crimes appear the lefs. In this refpect, inftead of *the facred hiftory of the Ifraelitifh nation being made profitable to them, for doctrine, for reproof, for correction, and for inftruction in righteoufnefs,* as it was intended, *and given to men* for that purpofe ; but, inftead thereof, the wars of the Ifraelites, the extirpation and fubjection of the Canaanites, and other tranfactions of that kind, are generally made ufe of by wicked men as precedents and pretences to encourage and embolden themfelves to commit cruelty and flavery on their fellow-creatures : and the mercilefs depredators, negociators, and enflavers of men, revert to the very ritual law of Mofes as a precedent for their barbarity, cruelty, and injuftice ; which law, though devoid of any iniquity, as bearing a parallel allufion to other things fignified thereby, can afford no precedent for their evil way, in any fhape or view : what was intended by it is fulfilled, and in no refpect,

or

or any thiug like it, can be repeated again, without tranfgreffing and breaking through every other injunction, precept, and command of the juft and tremendous law of God.

The confequence of their apoftacy from God, and difobedience to his law, became a fnare to thofe men in times of old, who departed from it ; and becaufe of their difobedience and wickednefs, the feveral nations, which went aftray after their own abominations, were vifited with many dreadful calamities and judgments. But to fet up the ways of the wicked for an example, and to make the laws refpecting their fuppreffion, and the judgments that were inflicted upon them for their iniquity, and even the written word of God, and the tranfactions of his providence, to be reverfed and become and precedents and pretences for men to commit depredations and extirpations, and for enflaving and negociating or merchandizing the human fpecies, muft be horrible wickednefs indeed, and finning with a high hand. And it cannot be thought otherwife, but that the abandoned aggreffors, among the learned nations will, in due time, as the juft reward of their aggravated iniquity, be vifited with fome more dreadful and tremendous judgments of the righteous vengeance of God, than what even befel to the Canaanites of old.

And it may be confidered further, that to draw any inferences in favour of extirpation, flavery, and negociation of men, from the written word of God, or from any thing elfe in the hiftory and cuftoms of different nations, as a precedent to embolden wicked men in their wickednefs ; cannot be more wicked, ridiculous, and abfurd to fhew any favour to thefe infidious negociators and

and enſlavers, than it would be to ſtand and laugh, and look on with a brutal and ſavage impunity, at beholding the following ſuppoſition tranſacted. Suppoſe two or three half-witted fooliſh fellows happened to come paſt a crowd of people, gazing at one which they had hung up by the neck on a tree, as a victim ſuffering for breaking the laws of his country ; and ſuppoſe theſe fooliſh fellows went on a little way in a bye path, and found ſome innocent perſon, not ſuſpecting any harm till taken hold of by them, and could not deliver-himſelf from them, and juſt becauſe they had ſeen among the crowd of people which they came paſt, that there had been a man hung by the neck, they took it into their fooliſh wicked heads to hang up the poor innocent man on the next tree, and juſt did as they had ſeen others do, to pleaſe their own fancy and baſe fooliſhneſs, to ſee how he would ſwing. Now if any of the other people happened to come up to them, and ſaw what they had done, would they heſitate a moment to determine between themſelves and theſe fooliſh raſcals which had done wickedneſs? Surely not ; they would immediately take hold of ſuch ſtupid wicked wretches, if it was in their power, and for their brutiſh fooliſhneſs, have them chained in a Bedlam, or hung on a gibbet. But what would theſe baſe fooliſh wretches ſay for themſelves ? That they ſaw others do ſo, and they thought there had been no harm in it, and they only did as they had ſeen the crowd of people do before. A poor fooliſh, baſe, raſcally excuſe indeed ! But not a better excuſe than this, can the brutiſh enſlavers and negociators of men find in all the annals of hiſtory. The enſnarers, negociators, and oppreſ-

ſors

fors of men, have only to become more abandoned in wickedness than these supposed wretches
could be; and to pass on in the most abominable bye paths of wickedness, and make every
thing that they can see an example for their
brutal barbarity; and whether it be a man
hanged for his crimes, or an innocent man for
the wretched wickedness of others; right or
wrong it makes no difference to them, if they
can only satisfy their own wretched and brutal
avarice. Whether it be the Israelites subjecting
the Canaanites for their crimes, or the Canaanites subjecting the Israelites, to gratify their own
wickedness, it makes no difference to them.
When they see some base wretches like themselves ensnaring, enslaving, oppressing, whip-
ping, starving with hunger, and cruelly torturing and murdering some of the poor helpless
part of mankind, they would think no harm in
it, they would do the same. Perhaps the Greeks
and Romans, and other crowds of barbarous nations have done so before; they can make that a
precedent, and think no harm in it, they would
still do the same, and worse than any barbarous
nations ever did before: and if they look back-
wards and forwards they can find no better precedent, ancient or modern, than that which is
wicked, mean, brutish, and base. To practise
such abominable parallels of wickedness of ensnaring, negociating, and enslaving men, is the
scandal and shame of mankind; And what must
we think of their crimes? Let the groans and
cries of the murdered, and the cruel slavery of
the Africans tell!

They that can stand and look on and behold
no evil in the infamous traffic of slavery must be

funk

funk to a wonderful degree of infenfibility; but furely thofe that can delight in that evil way for their gain, and be pleafed with the wickednefs of the wicked, and fee no harm in fubjecting their fellow-creatures to flavery, and keeping them in a ftate of bondage and fubjection as a brute, muft be wretchedly brutifh indeed. But fo bewitched are the general part of mankind with fome fottifh or felfifh principle, that they care nothing about what is right or wrong, any farther than their own intereft leads them to; and when avarice leads them on they can plead a thoufand excufes for doing wrong, or letting others do wickedly, fo as they have any advantage by it, to their own gratification and ufe. That fottifh and felfifh principle, without concern and difcernment among men is fuch, that if they can only profper themfelves, they care nothing about the miferable fituation of others: and hence it is, that even thofe who are elevated to high rank of power and affluence, and as becoming their eminent ftations, have opportunity of extending their views afar, yet they can fhut their eyes at this enormous evil of the flavery and commerce of the human fpecies; and, contrary to all the boafted accomplifhments, and fine virtues of the civilized and enlightened nations, they can fit ftill and let the torrent of robbery, flavery, and oppreffion roll on.

There is a way which feemeth good unto a man, but the end thereof are the ways of death. Should the enflavers of men think to juftify themfelves in their evil way, or that it can in any poffible way be right for them to fubject others to flavery; it is but charitable to evince and declare unto them, that they are thofe who have gone

into

into that evil way of brutifh ftupidity as well as wickednefs, that they can behold nothing of moral rectitude and equity among men but in the gloomy darknefs of their own hemifphere, like the owls and night-hawks, who can fee nothing but mift and darknefs in the meridian blaze of day. When men forfake the paths of virtue, righteoufnefs, juftice, and mercy, and become vitiated in any evil way, all their pretended virtues, fenfibility, and prudence among men, however high they may fhine in their own, and of others eftimation, will only appear to be but fpecious villainy at laft. That virtue which will ever do men any good in the end, is as far from that which fome men call fuch, as the gaudy appearance of a glow-worm in the dark is to the intrinfic value and luftre of a diamond : for if a man hath not love in his heart to his fellow-creatures, with a generous philanthropy diffufed throughout his whole foul, all his other virtues are not worth a ftraw.

The whole law of God is founded upon love, and the two grand branches of it are thefe : *Thou fhalt love the Lord thy God with all thy heart and with all thy foul ; and thou fhalt love thy neighbour as thyfelf.* And fo it was when man was firft created and made : they were created male and female, and pronounced to be in the image of God, and, as his reprefentative, to have dominion over the lower creation : and their Maker, who is love, and the intellectual Father of Spirits, bleffed them, and commanded them to arife in a bond of union of nature and of blood, each being a brother and a fifter together, and each the lover and the loved of one another. But when they were envied and invaded by the grand

enflaver

enflaver of men, all their jarring incoherency
arofe, and thofe who adhered to their pernicious
ufurper foon became envious, hateful, and ha-
ting one another. And thofe who go on to injure, enfnare, opprefs, and enflave their fellow-
creatures, manifeft their hatred to men, and
maintain their own infamous dignity and vaffalage, as the fervants of fin and the devil : but the
man that has any honour as a man fcorns their
ignominious dignity : the noble philanthropift
looks up to his God and Father as his only fovereign ; and he looks around on his fellow men as
his brethren and friends ; and in every fituation
and cafe, however mean and contemptible they
may feem, he endeavours to do them good : and
fhould he meet with one in the defert, whom he
never faw before, he would hail him my brother !
my fifter ! my friend ! how fares it with thee ?
And if he can do any of them any good it would
gladden every nerve of his foul.

But as there is but *one law and one manner* pre-
fcribed univerfally for all mankind, *for you, and
for the ftranger that fojourneth with you,* and wherefover they may be fcattered throughout the face
of the whole earth, the difference of fuperiority
and inferiority which are found fubfifting amongft
them is no way incompatible with the univerfal
law of love, honor, righteoufnefs, and equity ;
fo that a free, voluntary, and fociable fervitude,
which is the very bafis of human fociety, either
civil or religious, whereby we ferve one another
that we may be ferved, or do good that good
may be done unto us, is in all things requifite
and agreeable to all law and juftice. But the
taking away the natural liberties of men, and
compelling them to any involuntary flavery, or
compulfory

compulfory fervice, is an injury and robbery contrary to all law, civilization, reafon, juftice, equity, and humanity : therefore when men break through the laws of God, and the rules of civilization among men, and go forth to fteal, to rob, to plunder, to opprefs and to enflave, and to deftroy their fellow-creatures, the laws of God and man require that they fhould be fuppreffed, and deprived of their liberty, or perhaps their lives.

But juftice and equity does not always refide among men, even where fome confiderable degree of civilization is maintained ; if it had, that moft infamous refervoir of public and abandoned merchandizers and enflavers of men would not have been fuffered fo long, nor the poor unfortunate Africans, that never would have croffed the Atlantic to rob them, would not have become their prey. But it is juft as great and as heinous a tranfgreffion of the law of God to fteal, kidnap, buy, fell, and enflave any one of the Africans, as it would be to enfnare any other man in the fame manner, let him be who he will. And fuppofe that fome of the African pirates had been as dextrous as the Europeans, and that they had made excurfions on the coaft of Great-Britain or elfewhere, and though even affifted by fome of yonr own infiduous neighbours, for there may be fome men even among you vile enough to do fuch a thing if they could get money by it ; and that they fhould carry off your fons and your daughters, and your wives and friends, to a perpetual and barbarous flavery, you would certainly think that thofe African pirates were juftly deferving of any punifhment that could be put upon them. But the European pirates and
merchandizers

merchandizers of the human fpecies, let them belong to what nation they will, are equally as bad; and they have no better right to fteal, kid-nap, buy, and carry away and fell the Africans, than the Africans would have to carry away any of the Europeans in the fame barbarous and un-lawful manner.

But again, let us follow the European piracy to the Weft-Indies, or any where among Chrif-tians, and this law of the *Lord Chrift* muft flare every infidel flave-holder in the face, *And as ye would that men fhould do to you, do ye alfo to them likewife.* But there is no flave-holder would like to have himfelf enflaved, and to be treated as a dog, and fold like a beaft; and therefore the flave-holders, and merchandizers of men, tranf-grefs this plain law, and they commit a greater violation againft it, and act more contrary unto it, than it would be for a parcel of flaves to af-fume authority over their mafters, and compel them to flavery under them; for, if that was not doing as they would wifh to be done to, it would be doing, at leaft, as others do to them, in a way equally as much and more wrong. But our Di-vine Lord and *Mafter Chrift* alfo teacheth men to *forgive one another their trefpaffes,* and that we are not to do evil becaufe others do fo, and to re-venge injuries done unto us, Wherefore it is better, and more our duty, to offer ourfelves to be lafhed and cruelly treated, than to take up the tafk of their barbarity. The juft law of God re-quires an equal retaliation and reftoration for every injury that men may do to others, to fhew the greatnefs of the crime; but the law of for-bearance, righteoufnefs and forgivenefs, forbids the retaliation to be fought after, when it would

be

be doing as great an injury to them, without any reparation or benefit to ourselves. For what man can reftore an eye that he may have deprived ano her of, and if even a double punifhment was to pafs upon him, and that he was to lofe both his eyes for the crime, that would make no reparation to the other man whom he had deprived of one eye. And fo, likewife, when a man is carried captive and enflaved, and maimed and cruelly treated, that would make no adequate reparation and reftitution for the injuries he had received, if he was even to get the perfon who had enfnared him to be taken captive and treated in the fame manner. What he is to feek after is a deliverance and protection for himfelf, and not a revenge upon others. Wherefore the honeft and upright, like the juft Bethlehem Jofeph, cannot think of doing evil, nor require an equal retaliation for fuch injuries done to them, fo as to revenge themfelves upon others, for that which would do them no manner of good, Such vengeance belongeth unto the Lord, and he will render vengeance and recompence to his enemies and the violaters of his law.

But thus faith the law of God : *If a man be found ftealing any of his neighbours, or he that ftealeth a man (let him be who he will) and felleth him, or that maketh merchandize of him, or if he be found in his hand, then that thief fhall die.* However, in all modern flavery among Chriftians, who ought to know this law, they have not had any regard to it. Surely if any law among them admits of death as a punifhment for robbing or defrauding others of their money or goods, it ought to be double death; if it was poffible, when a man is robbed of himfelf, and fold into captivity and cruel

cruel flavery. But becaufe of his own goodnefs, and becaufe of the univerfal depravity of men, the Sovereign Judge of all has introduced a law of forbearance, to fpare fuch tranfgreffors, where in many cafes the law denounces death as the punifhment for their crimes, unlefs for thofe founded upon murder, or fuch abominations as cannot be forborn with in any civilization among men. But this law of forbearance is no alteration of the law itfelf; it is only a refpite in order to fpare fuch as will fly to him for refuge and forgivenefs for all their crimes, and for all their iniquities, who is the righteous fulfiller of the law, and the furety and reprefentative of men before God : and if they do not repent of their iniquity, and reform to a life of new obedience, as being under greater obligations to the law, but go on in their evil way, they muft at laft for ever lie under the curfe and every penalty of the juft and holy law of tht Moft High. This feems to be determined fo by that Great Judge of the law, when the accufers of a woman, taken in adultery, brought her before him, he ftooped down as a man and wrote, we may fuppofe, the crimes of her accufers in the duft, and as the God of all intelligence painted them in their confciences, wherefore they fled away one by one, and the woman was left alone before him; and as there was none of her accufers in that cafe righteous enough to throw the firft ftone, and to execute the law upon her, fhe was, Bid to go and fin no more. But it is manifeft that every crime that men may commit, where death is mentioned as the penalty thereof in the righteous law of God, it denotes a very great offence and a heinous trangreffion ; and although, in many cafes, it may

F   meet

meet with fome mitigation in the punifhment, becaufe of the forbearance of God, and the un-righteoufnefs of men, it cannot thereby be thought the lefs criminal in itfelf. But it alfo fuppofes, where ftrict feverities are made ufe of in the laws of civilization, that the doers of the law, and the judges of it, ought to be very righteous them-felves. And with regard to that law of men-ftealers, merchandizers, and of flaves found in their hands, that whatever mitigation and for-bearance fuch offenders ought to meet with, their crimes denote a very heinous offence, and a great violation of the law of God; they ought, there-fore, to be punifhed according to their trefpaffes, which, in fome cafes, fhould be death, if the perfon fo robbed and ftole fhould die in confe-quence thereof, or fhould not be reftored and brought back; and even then to be liable to every damage and penalty that the judges fhould think proper: for fo it is annexed to this law and required, *that men fhould put away evil from among them.* But this cannot now extend to the Weft-India flavery: what fhould rather be re-quired of them, in their prefent cafe of infatua-tion, is to furrender and give it up, and heal the ftripes that they have wounded, and to pour the healing balm of Chriftianity into the bleeding wounds of Heathen barbarity and cruelty.

All the criminal laws of civilization feem to be founded upon that law of God which was pub-lifhed to Noah and his fons; and, confequently, as it is again and again repeated, it becomes ir-reverfible, and univerfal to all mankind. *And furely your blood of your lives will I require: at the hand of every beaft will I require it; and at the hand of man, at the hand of every man's brother, will I require*

require the life of man. Whoso sheddeth man's blood, by man shall his blood be shed: for in the image of God made be man. If this law of God had not been given to men, murder itself would not have been any crime; and those who punished it with death would just have been as guilty as the other. But the law of God is juft, righteous and holy, and ought to be regarded and revered above all the laws of men; and this is added unto it: *What thing soever I command you, observe to do it: thou shalt not add thereto, nor diminish from it.* But it is an exceeding impious thing for men ever to presume, or think, as some will say, that they would make it death as a punishment for such a thing, and such a trespass; or that they can make any criminal laws of civilization as binding with a penalty of death for any thing just what they please. No such thing can be supposed; no man upon earth ever had, or ever can have, a right to make laws where a penalty of cutting off by death is required as the punishment for the transgression thereof: what is required of men is to be the doers of the law, and some of them to be judges of it; and if they judge wrongfully in taking away the lives of their fellow-creatures contrary to the law of God, they commit murder.

The reason why a man suffers death for breaking the laws of his country is, because he tranfgreffeth the law of God in that community he belongs to; and the laws of civilization are binding to put that law in force, and to point out and shew a sufficient warrant wherefore he should suffer, according as the just law of God requires for his trespass; and then it is just and right that

he

he fhould die for his crime. And as murder is irreverfibly to be punifhed with death, fometimes when it is not done, but only implied or eventually intended, it even then requires death; and in this fenfe it becomes right to face our enemies in the field of battle, and to cut them off. And when fpies and incendiaries rife up, or when rebellions break forth, and the lives of the Sovereign and others, and the good of the community is not fafe while fuch pretenders and their chief fupporters are fuffered to live; then it may be lawful, in fome cafes, that they fhould die; but in cafes of this kind there is generally more cowardice and cruelty than juftice and mercy regarded, and more difcretionary power left for men to ufe their authority in, and to eftablifh criminal laws or precedents than in any thing elfe. Hence we may find many of the different chiefs and kings in different parts of the world, in all ages, wading through a fea of blood to their thrones, or fupporting themfelves upon it, by defolating and deftroying others; and we may find good and bad in all ages fetting up wretched examples for men to be guided by; and herein we may find a David, a Solomon, a Cromwell, committing murder and death, and a Charles the Second committing a greater carnage upon more innocent people than thofe who fuffered in the reign of a bloody Queen Mary; and even in a late rebellion there were many fuffered in Britain, which, if they had been preferved to this mild reign, they would have been as good neighbours, and as faithful fubjects, as any other. But among all pretences for taking away the lives of men by any form of law, that for religion is the moft
unwar-

unwarrantable: it is the command of God to
fupprefs idolatry, and to break down the images
and external pomp of grofs fuperftition, but not
to deftroy men themfelves: that perfecution is
murder if it takes away the lives of men for
their religion, for it has nothing to do with what
men may think with refpect to their own duty;
and if a man is foolifh enough to make an image
of wood or ftone, and to worfhip it, or even to
adore a picture, if he keeps it to himfelf, perfecution has nothing to do with him.

The law of God forbids all manner of covetoufnefs and theft: but when any thing is taken
away by ftealth, it is not like thofe injuries which
cannot be reftored, as the cutting off or wounding any of the members of the body; but it admits of a poffible reftoration, whether the viola-
tors can reftore it or not as the law requires, fo
if a man owes a juft debt it is not the lefs due
by him if he has got nothing to pay it with;
fuch trangreffors ought to be punifhed according
to their trefpaffes, but not with death: for the
law of God is, " If a thief be found breaking up,
" and he be fmitten that he die, if it was in the
" night there fhall be no blood fhed for him;
" but if the fun be rifen upon him, there was
" blood required for him if he was killed; for
" faith the law it required only he fhould make
" full reftitution; and if he had nothing, then
" he fhould be fold for his theft. And if any
" manner of theft be found in a man's hand, the
" law requires a retaliation and reftoration; that
" is, that he fhould reftore double; but if it be
" fold or made away with, it was then to be four-
" fold, and, in fome cafes, five, fix or feven times

F 3   " as

" as much *." According to this law, when the property of others is taken away, either by ftealth, fraud, or violence, the aggreffors fhould be fubjected to fuch bondage and hard labour, (and efpecially when the trefpafs is great, and they have nothing to pay) as would be requifite to make reftitution to the injured, and to bring about a reformation to themfelves. And if they have committed violence either by threats or force, they ought to fuffer bodily punifhment, and the feverity of it according to their crimes, and the ftubbornnefs of their obduracy ; and all fuch punifhments as are neceffary fhould be inflicted upon them without pitying or fparing them, though perhaps not to be continued for ever in the brutal manner that the Weft-India flaves fuffer for almoft no crimes.

But whereas the robbing of others in any manner of their property is often attended with fuch cruelty and violence, and a fevere lofs to the fufferers, it may, in fome cafes, be thought that the law of God fufficiently warrants the taking away the lives of the aggreffors ; for the taking away of a man's property in general may be confidered as taking away his life, or at leaft the means of his fupport, and then the punifhing the tranfgreffors with death can only in that cafe be reckoned a conftructive murder. Wherefore the tranfgreffors ought to be punifhed feverely ; but never with any laws of civilization where death is concerned, without a regard to the law of God.

* A great part of this law is ftrictly obferved in Africa, and we make ufe of facrifices, and keep a fabbath every feventh day, more ftrictly than Chriftians generally do.

And

And when the law of God admits of a forbearance, and a kind of forgivenefs in many things,
it ought to be the grand law of civilization to
feek out fuch rules of punifhment as are beft cal-
culated to prevent injuries of every kind, and to
reclaim the tranfgreffors ; and it is beft, if it can
be done, to punifh with a lefs degree of feverity
than their crimes deferve. But all the laws of
civilization muft jar greatly when the law of God
is fcrewed up in the greateft feverity to punifh
men for their crimes on the one hand, and on
the other to be totally difregarded*. When the
Divine law points out a theft, where the thief
fhould make reftitution for his trefpafs, the laws
of civilization fay, he muft die for his crime :
and when that law tells us, that he who ftealeth
or maketh merchandize of men, that fuch a thief
fhall furely die, the laws of civilization fay, in
many cafes, that it is no crime. In this the ways
of men are not equal ; but let the wife and juft
determine whether the laws of God or the laws of
men are right.

Amongft fome of the greateft tranfgreffors of
the laws of civilization, thofe that defraud the
public by forgery, or by fubftituting or falfifying
any of the current fpecie, ought to have their
lives or their liberties taken away ; for although
they may not do any perfonal injury, they commit
the greateft robbery and theft, both to individuals and the whole community. But even in the
fuppreffion of thofe, men have no right to add or

* This confeffional minftrel may be often repeated, but, I
fear, feldom regarded : " We have offended againft thy holy
" laws ; we have left undone thofe things which we ought to
" have done ; and we have done thofe things which we
" ought not to have done."

diminifh

diminſh any thing to the law of God, with reſpect
to taking away their lives. Wherefore, if the law
of God does not ſo clearly warrant, that they
ſhould die for their theft, it, at leaſt, fully warrants that they ſhould be ſold into ſlavery for
their crimes; and the laws of civilization may
juſtly bind them, and hold them in perpetual
bondage, becauſe they have ſold themſelves to
work iniquity; but not that they ſhould be ſold
to the heathen, or to ſuch as would not inſtruct
them : for there might be hope, that if good inſtruction was properly adminiſtered unto them,
there might be a poſſible reformation wrought
upon ſome of them. Some, by their ingenious
aſſiduity, have tamed the moſt ſavage wild beaſts;
it is certainly more laudable to tame the moſt
brutiſh and ſavage men, and, in time, there might
be ſome Oneſimus's found amongſt them, that
would become uſeful to reclaim others. Thoſe
that break the laws of civilization, in any flagrant
manner, are the only ſpecies of men that others
have a right to enſlave; and ſuch ought to be ſold
to the community, with every thing that can be
found belonging to them, to make a commutation of reſtitution as far as could be; and they
ſhould be kept at ſome uſeful and laborious employment, and it might be at ſome embankation,
or recovering of waſte ground, as there might be
land recovered on rivers and ſhores, worth all the
expence, for the benefit of the community they
belonged to. The continuance of that criminal
ſlavery and bondage, ought to be according to the
nature of their crimes, with a reference to their
good behaviour, either to be continued or pro-
tracted. Such as were condemned for life, when
their crimes were great, and themſelves ſtubborn,
might

might be fo marked as to render their getting away impoffible without being difcovered, and that the very fight of one of them might deter others from committing their crimes, as much as hanging perhaps a dozen of them; and it might be made fo fevere unto them, that it would render their own fociety in bondage, almoft the only preferable one that they could enjoy among men. The manner of confining them would not be fo impracticable as fome may be apt to think; and all thefe feverities come under the laws of men to punifh others for their crimes, but they fhould not go beyond the juft law of God; and neither fhould his laws be fufpended, where greater trefpaffes are committed.

In this fenfe every free community might keep flaves, or criminal prifoners in bondage; and fhould they be fold to any other, it fhould not be to ftrangers, nor without their own confent; and if any were fold for a term of years, they would naturally become free as foon as their purchafe could be paid. But if any man fhould buy another man without his own confent, and compel him to his fervice and flavery without any agreement of that man to ferve him, the enflaver is a robber, and a defrauder of that man every day. Wherefore it is as much the duty of a man who is robbed in that manner to get out of the hands of his enflaver, as it is for any honeft community of men to get out of the hands of rogues and villains. And however much is required of men to forgive one another their trefpaffes in one refpect, it is alfo manifeft, and what we are commanded, as noble, to refift evil in another, in order to prevent others doing evil, and to keep ourfelves from harm. Therefore, if there was no other way to deliver a

man

man from flavery, but by enflaving his mafter, it
would be lawful for him to do fo if he was able,
for this would be doing juftice to himfelf, and be
juftice, as the law requires, to chaftife his mafter
for enflaving of him wrongfully.

Thence this general and grand duty fhould be
obferved by every man, not to follow the multitude to do evil, neither to recompence evil for
evil; and yet, fo that a man may lawfully defend
himfelf, and endeavour to fecure himfelf, and
others, as far as he can, from injuries of every
kind. Wherefore all along, in the hiftory of
mankind, the various depredations committed in
the world, by enflaving, extirpating and deftroying men, were always contrary to the laws of
God, and what he had ftrictly forbidden and commanded not to be done. But infolent, proud,
wicked men, in all ages, and in all places, are
alike; they difregard the laws of the Moft High,
and ftop at no evil in their power, that they can
contrive with any pretence of confiftency in doing
mifchief to others, fo as it may tend to promote
their own profit and ambition. Such are all the
depredators, kidnappers, merchandizers and enflavers of men; they do not care, nor confider,
how much they injure others, if they can make
any advantage to themfelves by it. But whenever
thefe things were committed by wicked men, a
retaliation was fought after, as the only way of
deliverance; for he who leadeth into captivity,
fhould be carried captive; and he which deftroy-
eth with the fword, fhould die with the fword.
And as it became neceffary to punifh thofe that
wronged others, when the punifhers went beyond
the bounds of a juft retaliation, and fell into the
fame crimes of the oppreffors, not to prevent
them-

themselves from harm, and to deliver the oppressed and the captive, but to oppress and enslave others, as much as they before them had done, the consequence is plain, that an impending overthrow must still fall upon them likewise. In that respect, so far as conquerors are permitted to become a judgment and a scourge to others, for their enormous transgressions, they are themselves not a bit the more safe, for what they do, they often do wickedly for their own purpose; and when the purpose of Divine Providence, who raised them up, is fulfilled by them, in the punishment of others for their crimes; the next wave thereof will be to visit them also according to their wickedness with some dreadful overthrow, and to swallow them up in the sea of destruction and oblivion.

History affords us many examples of severe retaliations, revolutions and dreadful overthrows; and of many crying under the heavy load of subjection and oppression, seeking for deliverance. And methinks I hear now, many of my countrymen, in complexion, crying and groaning under the heavy yoke of slavery and bondage, and praying to be delivered; and the word of the Lord is thus speaking for them, while they are bemoaning themselves under the grievous bonds of their misery and woe, saying, *Woe is me! alas Africa! for I am as the last gleanings of the summer fruit, as the grape gleanings of the vintage, where no cluster is to eat. The good are perished out of the earth, and there is none upright among men; they all lie in wait for blood; they hunt every man his brother with a net. That they may do evil with both hands earnestly, the prince asketh, and the judge asketh for a reward; and the great man he uttereth his mischievous desire:*

defire: fo they wrap it up. Among *the beft* in Africa, we have found them *fharp as a briar;* among *the moft upright,* we have found them *fharper than a thorn-hedge* in the Weft-Indies. Yet, O Africa! yet, poor flave! *The day of thy watchmen cometh, and thy vifitation* draweth nigh, *that fhall be their perplexity. Therefore I will look unto the Lord; I will wait for the God of my falvation; my God will hear me. Rejoice not againft me, O mine enemy; though I be fallen, I fhall yet arife; though I fit in darknefs, the Lord fhall yet be a light unto me. I will bear the indignation of the Lord, becaufe I have finned againft him, until he plead my caufe, and execute judgment for me, and I fhall behold his righteoufnefs. Then mine enemies fhall fee it, and fhame fhall cover them which:faid unto me, Where is the Lord thy God,* that regardeth thee: *Mine eyes fhall behold them trodden down as the mire of the ftreets. In that day that thy walls* of deliverance *are to be built, in that day fhall the decree* of flavery *be far removed.*

What revolution the end of that predominant evil of flavery and oppreffion may produce, whether the wife and confiderate will furrender and give it up, and make reftitution for the injuries that they have already done, as far as they can; or whether the force of their wickednefs, and the iniquity of their power, will lead them on until fome univerfal calamity burft forth againft the abandoned carriers of it on, and againft the criminal nations in confederacy with them, is not for me to determine? But this muft appear evident, that for any man to carry on a traffic in the merchandize of flaves, and to keep them in flavery; or for any nation to opprefs, extirpate and deftroy others; that thefe are crimes of the greateft magnitude,

magnitude, and a moſt daring violation of the laws and commandments of the Moſt High, and which, at laſt, will be evidenced in the deſtruction and overthrow of all the tranſgreſſors. And nothing elſe can be expected for ſuch violations of taking away the natural rights and liberties of men, but that thoſe who are the doers of it will meet with ſome awful viſitation of the righteous judgment of God, and in ſuch a manner as it cannot be thought that his juſt vengeance for their iniquity will be the leſs tremendous becauſe his judgments are long delayed.

None but men of the moſt brutiſh and depraved nature, led on by the invidious influence of infernal wickedneſs, could have made their ſettlements in the different parts of the world diſcovered by them, and have treated the various Indian nations, in the manner that the barbarous inhuman Europeans have done : and their eſtabliſhing and carrying on that moſt diſhoneſt, unjuſt and diabolical traffic of buying and ſelling, and of enſlaving men, is ſuch a monſtrous, audacious and unparallelled wickedneſs, that the very idea of it is ſhocking, and the whole nature of it is horrible and infernal. It may be ſaid with confidence as a certain general fact, that all their foreign ſettlements and colonies were founded on murders and devaſtations, and that they have continued their depredations in cruel ſlavery and oppreſſion to this day : for where ſuch predominant wickedneſs as the African ſlave-trade, and the Weſt Indian ſlavery, is admitted, tolerated and ſupported by them, and carried on in their colonies, the nations and people who are the ſupporters and encouragers thereof muſt be not only guilty themſelves of that ſhameful and abandoned

doned evil and wickednefs, fo very difgraceful to human nature, but even partakers in thofe crimes of the moft vile combinations of various pirates, kidnappers, robbers and thieves, the ruffians and ftealers of men, that ever made their appearance in the world.

Soon after Columbus had difcovered America, that great navigator was himfelf greatly embarraffed and treated unjuftly, and his beft defigns counteracted by the wicked bafenefs of thofe whom he led to that difcovery. The infernal conduct of his Spanifh competitors, whofe leading motives were covetoufnefs, avarice and fanaticifm, foon made their appearance, and became cruel and dreadful. At Hifpaniola the bafe perfidy and bloody treachery of the Spaniards, led on by the perfidious Ovando, in feizing the peaceable Queen Anacoana and her attendants, burning her palace, putting all to deftruction, and the innocent Queen and her people to a cruel death, is truly horrible and lamentable. And led on by the treacherous Cortes, the fate of the great Montezuma was dreadful and fhocking; how that American monarch was treated, betrayed and deftroyed, and his vaft extenfive empire of the Mexicans brought to ruin and devaftation, no man of fenfibility and feeling can read the hiftory without pity and refentment. And looking over another page of that hiftory, fenfibility would kindle into horror and indignation, to fee the bafe treacherous baftard Pizarra at the head of the Spanifh banditti of mifcreant depredators, leading them on, and overturning one of the moft extenfive empires in the world. To recite a little of this as a fpecimen of the reft: It feems Pizarra, with his company of depredators,

tors, had artfully penetrated into the Peruvian empire, and pretended an embaſſy of peace from a great monarch, and demanded an audience of the noble Atahualpa, the great Inca or Lord of that empire, that the terms of their embaſſy might be explained, and the reaſon of their coming into the territories of that monarch. Atahualpa fearing the menaces of thoſe terrible invaders, and thinking to appeaſe them by complying with their requeſt, relied on Pizarra's feigned pretenſions of friendſhip; accordingly the day was appointed, and Atahualpa made his appearance with the greateſt decency and ſplendor he could, to meet ſuch ſuperior beings as the Americans conceived their invaders to be, with four hundred men in an uniform dreſs, as harbingers to clear the way before him, and himſelf ſitting on a throne or couch, adorned with plumes of various colours, and almoſt covered with plates of gold and ſilver, enriched with precious ſtones, and was carried on the ſhoulders of his principal attendants. As he approached near the Spaniſh quarters the arch fanatic Father Vincent Valverde, chaplain to the expedition, advanced with a crucifix in one hand and a breviary in the other, and began with a long diſcourſe, pretending to explain ſome of the general doctrines of Chriſtianity, together with the fabulous notion of St. Peter's vicegerency, and the tranſmiſſion of his apoſtolic power continued in the ſucceſſion of the Popes; and that the then Pope, Alexander, by donation, had inveſted their maſter as the ſole Monarch of all the New World. In conſequence of this, Atahualpa was inſtantly required to embrace the Chriſtian religion, acknowledge the juriſdiction of the

Pope,

Pope, and fubmit to the Great Monarch of Caf-
tile ; but if he fhould refufe an immediate com-
pliance with thefe requifitions, they were to declare war againft him, and that he might expect
the dreadful effects of their vengeance. This
ftrange harangue, unfolding deep myfteries, and
alluding to fuch unknown facts, of which no
power of eloquence could tranflate, and convey,
at once, a diftinct idea to an American, that its
general tenor was altogether incomprehenfible to
Atahualpa. Some parts in it, as more obvious
than the reft, filled him with aftonifhment and
indignation. His reply, however, was temperate, and as fuitable as could be well expected.
He obferved that he was Lord of the dominions
over which he reigned by hereditary fucceffion ;
and, faid, that he could not conceive how a foreign prieft fhould pretend to difpofe of territories
which did not belong to him, and that if fuch
a prepofterous grant had been made, he, who
was the rightful poffeffor, refufed to confirm it;
that he had no inclination to renounce the religious inftitutions eftablifhed by his anceftors;
nor would he forfake the fervice of the Sun, the
immortal divinity whom he and his people revered, in order to worfhip the God of the Spaniards, who was fubject to death; and that with
refpect to other matters, he had never heard of
them before, and did not then underftand their
meaning. And he defired to know where Valverde had learned things fo extraordinary. In
this book, replied the fanatic Monk, reaching
out his breviary. The Inca opened it eagerly,
and turning over the leaves, lifted it to his ear :
This, fays he, is filent ; it tell tells me nothing;
and threw it with difdain to the ground. The
enraged

enraged father of ruffians, turning towards his countrymen, the affaffinators, cried out, To arms, Chriftians, to arms ; the word of God is infulted ; avenge this profanation on thefe impious dogs.

At this the Chriftian defperadoes impatient in delay, as foon as the fignal of affault was given their martial mufic began to play, and their attack was rapid, rufhing fuddenly upon the Peruvians, and with their hell-invented enginery of thunder, fire and fmoke, they foon put them to flight and deftruction. The Inca. though his nobles crouded round him with officious zeal, and fell in numbers at his feet, while they vied one with another in facrificing their own lives that they might cover the facred perfon of their Sovereign, was foon penetrated to by the affaffinators, dragged from his throne, and carried to the Spanifh quarters. The fate of the Monarch increafed the precipitate flight of his followers ; the plains being covered with upwards of thirty thoufand men, were purfued by the ferocious Spaniards towards every quarter, who, with deliberate and unrelenting barbarity, continued to flaughter the wretched fugitives till the clofe of the day, that never had once offered at any refiftance. Pizarra had contrived this daring and perfidious plan on purpofe to get hold of the Inca, notwithftanding his affumed character of an ambaffador from a powerful monarch to court an alliance with that prince, and in violation of all the repeated offers of his own friendfhip. The noble Inca thus found himfelf betrayed and fhut up in the Spanifh quarters, though fcarce aware at firft of the vaft carnage and deftruction of his people ; but foon conceiving the deftruc-

G   tive

tive confequences that attended his confinement, and by beholding the vaft treafures of fpoil that the Spaniards had fo eagerly gathered up, he learned fomething of their covetous difpo-fition : and he offered as a ranfom what afto-nifhed the Spaniards, even after all they now knew concerning the opulence of his kingdom : the apartment in which he was confined was twenty-two feet in length and fixteen in breadth, he undertook to fill it with veffels of gold as high as he could reach. This tempting propofal was eagerly agreed to by Pizarra, and a line was drawn upon the walls of the chamber to mark the ftipulated height to which the treafure was to rife. The gold was accordingly collected from various parts with the greateft expedition by the Inca's obedient and loving fubjects, who thought nothing too much for his ranfom and life ; but, after all, poor Atahualpa was cruelly murdered, and his body burnt by a military in-quifition, and his extenfive and rich dominions devoted to deftruction and ruin by thefe merci-lefs depredators.

The hiftory of thofe dreadfully perfidious me-thods of forming fettlements, and acquiring riches and territory, would make humanity tremble, and even recoil, at the enjoyment of fuch ac-quifitions and become reverted into rage and in-dignation at fuch horrible injuftice and barba-rous cruelty, " It is faid by the Peruvians, that " their Incas, or Monarchs, had uniformly ex-" tended their power with attention to the good " of their fubjects, that they might diffufe the " bleffings of civilization, and the knowledge of " the arts which they poffeffed, among the people " that embraced their protection; and during a
" fucceffion

" fucceſſion of twelve monarchs, not one had
" deviated from this beneficent character." Their
fenfibility of fuch noblenefs of character would
give them the moſt poignant diſlike to their new
terrible invaders that had defolated and laid
waſte their country. The character of their monarchs would feeem to vie with as great virtues
as any King in Europe can boaſt of Had the
Peruvians been vifited by men of honeſty, knowledge, and enlightened underſtanding, to teach
them, by patient inſtruction and the bleſſing of
God, they might have been induced to embrace
the doctrines and faith of Chriſtianity, and to
abandon their errors of fuperſtition and idolatry.
Had Chriſtians, that deferve the name thereof,
been fent among them, the many ufeful things
that they would have taught them, together with
their own pious example, would have captivated
their hearts; and the knowledge of the truth
would have made it a very defirous thing for the
Americans to have thofe that taught them to fet-
tle among them. Had that been the cafe the
Americans, in various parts, would have been
as eager to have the Europeans to come there as
they would have been to go, fo that the Europeans might have found fettlements enough, in a
friendly alliance with the inhabitants, without
deſtroying and enſlaving them. And had that
been the cafe, it might be fuppofed, that Europe
and America, long before now, would both
with a growing luxuriancy, have been flouriſhing
with affluence and peace, and their long extended
and fruitful branches, loaden with benents to
each other, reaching over the ocean, might have
been more extenfive, and greater advantages
have been expected, for the good of both than

G 2　　　　　　　　what

what has yet appeared. But, alas! at that time there was no Chriftians to fend,) and very few now), thefe were obliged to hide themfelves in the obfcure places of the earth; that was, according to Sir Ifaac Newton, to mix in obfcurity among the meaneft of the people, having no power and authority; and it feems at that time there was no power among Chriftians on earth to have fent fuch as would have been ufeful to the Americans; if there had they would have fent after the depredators, and refcued the innocent.

But as I faid before, it is furely to the great fhame and fcandal of Chriftianity among all the Heathen nations, that thofe robbers, plunderers, deftroyers and enflavers of men fhould call themfelves Chriftians, and exercife their power under any Chriftian government and authority. I would have my African countrymen to know and underftand, that the deftroyers and enflavers of men can be no Chriftians; for Chriftianity is the fyftem of benignity and love, and all its votaries are devoted to honefty, juftice, humanity, meeknefs, peace and good-will to all men. But whatever title or claim fome may affume to call themfelves by it, without poffeffing any of its virtues, can only manifeft them to be the more abominable liars, and the greateft enemies unto it, and as belonging to the fynagogue of Satan, and not the adherers to Chrift. For the enflavers and oppreffors of men, among thofe that have obtained the name of Chriftians, they are ftill acting as its greateft enemies, and contrary to all its genuine principles; they fhould therefore be called by its oppofite, the Antichrift. Such are fitly belonging to that moft diffolute forcerefs of all religion in the world:

" With

" With whom the kings of the earth have lived
" delicioufly ; and the inhabitants of the earth
" have been made drunk with the wine of
" her abominations ; and the merchants of the
" earth are waxed rich through the abundance
" of her delicacies, by their traffic in various
" things, and in flaves and fouls of men !"
It was not enough for the malignant deftroyer of
the world to fet up his hydra-headed kingdom
of evil and wickednefs among the kingdom of
men; but alfo to caufe an image to be made
unto him, by fomething imported in the only
true religion that ever was given to men ; and
that image of iniquity is defcribed as arifing up
out of the earth, having two horns like a lamb,
which, by its votaries and adherents, has been
long eftablifhed and fupported. One of its umbragious horns of apoftacy and delufion is founded, in a more particular refpect, on a grand perverfion of the Old Teftament difpenfations, which
has extended itfelf over all the Mahometan nations in the Eaft ; and the other horn of apoftacy, bearing an alliufion and profeffional refpect
to that of the new, has extended itfelf over all
the Chriftian nations in the Weft. That grand
umbragious fhadow and image of evil and wickednefs, has fpread its malignant influence over
all the nations of the earth, and has, by its power
of delufion, given countenance and fupport to all
the power of evil and wickednefs done among
men ; and all the adherents and fupporters of
that delufion, and all the carriers on of wickednefs, are fitly called Antichrift. But all the nations have drunk of the wine of that iniquity,
and become drunk with the wine of the wrath
of her fornication, whofe name, by every mark

and

and feature, is the Antichrift; and every dealer in flaves, and thofe that hold them in flavery, whatever elfe they may call themfelves, or whatever elfe they may profefs. And likewife, thofe nations whofe governments fupport that evil and wicked traffic of flavery, however r mote the fituation where it is carried on may be, are, in that refpect, as much Antichriftian as any thing in the world can be. No man will ever rob another unlefs he be a villain : nor will any nation or people ever enflave and opprefs others, unlefs themfelves be bafe and wicked men, and who act and do contrary and againft every duty in Chriftianity.

The learned and ingenious author of Britannia Libera, as chiefly alluding to Great-Britain alone, gives fome account of that great evil and wickednefs carried on by the Chriftian nations, refpecting the direful effects of the great devaftations committed in foreign parts, whereby it would appear that the ancient and native inhabitants have been drenched in blood and oppreffion by their mercilefs vifitors (which have formed colonies and fettlements among them) the avaricious depredators, plunderers and deftroyers of nations. As fome eftimate of it, " to deftroy " eleven million, and diftrefs many more in Ame- " rica, to ftarve and opprefs twelve million in " Afia, and the great number deftroyed, is not " the way to promote the dignity, ftrength and " fafety of empire, but to draw down the Di- " vine vengeance on the offenders, for depriving " fo many of their fellow-creatures of life, or the " common bleffings of the earth : whereas by " obferving the humane principles of preferva- " tion with felicitation, the proper principles of
                                                    " all

" all rulers, their empire might have received all
" reasonable benefit, with the encrease of future
" glory." But should it be asked, what advantages Great-Britain has gained by all its extensive
territories abroad, the devastations committed,
and the abominable slavery and oppression carried on in its colonies ? It may be answered according to the old proverb,

    It seldom is the grand-child's lot,
    To share of wealth unjustly got.

This seems to be verified too much in their pre-
sent situation : for however wide they have extended their territories abroad, they have sunk
into a world of debt at home, which must ever
remain an impending burden upon the inhabitants. And it is not likely, by any plan as yet
adopted, to be ever paid, or any part of it,
without a long continued heavy annual load of
taxes. Perhaps, great as it is some other plan,
more equitable for the good of the whole community, if it was wanted to be done, and without any additional taxes, might be so made use
of to pay it all off in twenty or thirty years time,
and in such manner as whatever emergencies
might happen, as never to need to borrow any
money at interest. The national debt casts a
sluggish deadness over the whole realm, greatly
stops ingenuity and improvements, promotes idle-
ness and wickedness, clogs all the wheels of commerce, and drains the money out of the nation.
If a foreigner buys stock, in the course of years
that the interest amounts to the principal, he gets
it all back ; and in an equitable time the same
sum ever after, and in course must take that
money to foreign parts. And those who hold
stock at home, are a kind of idle drones, as a
                                 burden

burden to the reft of the community : whereas
if there were no funds, thofe who have money
would be obliged to occupy it in fome improvements themfelves, or lend it to other manufac-
turers or merchants, and by that means ufeful
employments, ingenuity and commerce would
flourish. But all ftock-jobbing, lotteries, and
ufelefs bufinefs, has a tendency to flavery and
oppreffion; for as the greater any idle part of
the community is, there muft be the greater
labour and hardfhips refting upon the induftrious
part who fupport the reft; as all men are al-
lotted in fome degree to eat their bread with the
fweat of their brow; *but it is evil with any people
when the rich grind the face of the poor.* Lotteries muft be nearly as bad a way of getting money for the good of a nation, as it is for an individual when he is poor, and obliged to pawn
his goods to increafe his poverty, already poor.
On the reverfe, if a nation was to keep a bank
to lend money to merchants and others, that nation might flourifh, and its fupport to thofe in
need might be attended with advantage to the
whole; but that nation which is obliged to borrow money from others, muft be in a poor and
wretched fituation, and the inhabitants, who have
to bear the load of its taxes, muft be greatly
burdened, and perhaps many of thofe employed
in its fervice (as foldiers and others) poorly paid.
It was otherwife with *the people of Ifrael of old*;
it was the promife and blefling of God to them,
*That they fhould lend unto many nations, but fhould
not borrow.*

But when a nation or people do wickedly, and
commit cruelties and devaftations upon others,
and enflave them, it cannot be expected that they
fhould

should be attended with the bleffings of God, neither to efchew evil. They often become infatuated to do evil unawares ; and thofe employed under their fervice fometimes lead them into debt, error and wickednefs, in order to enrich themfelves by their plunder, in committing the moft barbarous cruelties, under pretences of war, wherein they were the firft aggreffors, and which is generally the cafe in all unnatural and deftructive difputes of war.   In this bufinefs money is wanted, the national debt becomes increafed, and new loans and other fums muft be added to the funds. The plunderers abroad fend home their cafh as faft as they can, and by one means and another the fums wanted to borrow, are foon made up. At laft when the wars fubfide, or other bufinefs calls them home, laden with the fpoils of the Eaft or elfewhere, they have then the grand part of their bufinefs to negociate, in buying up bank ftock, and lodging their plunder and ill-got wealth in the Britifh or other funds. Thus the nation is loaded with more debt, and with an annual addition of more intereft to pay, to the further advantage of thofe who often occafioned it by their villainy ; who, if they had their deferts, like the Popifh inquifitors, are almoft the only people in the world who deferve to be hung on the rack.

But fo it happens in general, that men of activity and affluence, by whatever way they are poffeffed of riches, or have acquired a greatnefs of fuch property, they are always preferred to take the lead in matters of government, fo that the greateft depredators, warriors, contracting companies of merchants, and rich flave-holders, always endeavour to pufh themfelves on to get

power

power and intereſt in their favour; that whatever crimes any of them commit they are ſeldom
brought to a juſt puniſhment. Unleſs that ſomething of this kind had been the caſe, 'tis impoſſible to conceive how ſuch an enormous evil as
the ſlave-trade could have been eſtabliſhed and
carried on under any Chriſtian government: and
from hence that motly ſyſtem of government,
which hath ſo ſprung up and eſtabliſhed itſelf,
may be accounted for, and as being an evident
and univerſal depravity of one of the fineſt con-
ſtitutions in the world; and it may be feared if
theſe unconſtitutional laws, reaching from Great-
Britain to her colonies, be long continued in
and ſupported, to the carrying on that horrible
and wicked traffic of ſlavery, muſt at laſt mark
out the whole of the Britiſh conſtitution with ruin
and deſtruction; and that the moſt generous and
tenacious people in the world for liberty, may
alſo at laſt be reduced to ſlaves. And an Ethiopian may venture to aſſert, that ſo long as ſlavery is continued in any part of the Britiſh dominions, that more than one-half of the legiſlature are the virtual ſupporters and encouragers
of a traffic which ought to be aboliſhed, as it
cannot be carried on but by ſome of the moſt
abandoned and profligate men upon earth.

However, the partizans of ſuch a claſs of men
are generally too many and numerous, whoſe
viciated principles from time to time have led the
whole nation into debt, error and diſgrace; and
by their magnetic influence there is a general
ſupport given to deſpotiſm, oppreſſion and cruelty. For many have acquired great riches by
ſome inſidious traffic or illegal gain; and as theſe
become often leading men in governments, vaſt
multitudes

multitudes by fea and land purfue the fame
courfe, and fupport the fame meafures; like adventurers in the lottery, each grafping for the
higheft prize; or as much enamoured with any
infamous way of getting riches, as the Spaniards
were with the Peruvian veffels of gold. And
when ambitious and wicked men are bent upon
avarice and covetoufnefs, it leads them on to
commit terrible cruelties, and their hearts become hardened in wickednefs; fo that even their
enormous crimes fink in their own eftimation,
and foften into trivial matters. The houfe-
breakers and highwaymen, petty depredators,
think nothing of any mifchief or cruelty that they
can do, fo as they can gain their end and come off
fafe; but their villainy and crimes appear to
other men as they ought to do, and if they can
be detected, and taken hold of, they will meet
with fuch punifhment as they juftly deferve for
their crimes. But it is otherwife with the Colo-
nians, the great depredators, pirates, kidnappers,
robbers, oppreffors and enflavers of men. The
laws as reaching from Great-Britain to the Weft-
Indies, do not detect them but protect the opulent flave-holders; though their opulence and
protection by any law, or any government whatfoever, cannot make them lefs criminal than vio-
lators of the common rights and liberties of men.
They do not take away a man's property, like
other robbers; but they take a man himfelf, and
fubject him to their fervice and bondage, which
is a greater robbery, and a greater crime, than
taking away any property from men whatfoever.
And, therefore, with refpect to them, there is
very much wanted for regulating the natural
rights of mankind, and very much wrong in the
prefent

prefent forms of government, as well as much abufe of that which is right.

The Spaniards began their fettlements in the Weft Indies and America, by depredations of rapine, injuftice, treachery and murder; and they have continued in the barbarous practice of devaftation, cruelty, and oppreffion ever fince: and their principles and maxims in planting colonies have been adopted, in fome meafure, by every other nation in Europe. This guiltful method of colonization muft undoubtedly and imperceptibly have hardened men's hearts, and led them on from one degree of barbarity and cruelty to another : for when they had deftroyed, wafted and defolated the native inhabitants, and when many of their own people, enriched with plunder, had retired, or returned home to enjoy their ill-gotten wealth, other refources for men to labour and cultivate the ground, and fuch other laborious employments were wanted. Vaft territories and large poffeffions, without getting inhabitants to labour for them, were of no ufe. A general part of what remained of the wretched fugitives, who had the beft native right to thofe poffeffions, were obliged to make their efcape to places more remote, and fuch as could not, were obliged to fubmit to the hard labour and bondage of their invaders; but as they had not been ufed to fuch harfh treatment and laborious employment as they were then fubjected to, they were foon wafted away and became few. Their proud invaders found the advantage of having their labour done for nothing, and it became their general practice to pick up the unfortunate ftrangers that fell in their way, when they thought they could make ufe of them in their fervice.
That

That bafe traffic of kidnapping and ftealing men was begun by the Portuguefe on the coaft of Africa, and as they found the benefit of it for their own wicked purpofes, they foon went on to commit greater depredations. The Spaniards followed their infamous example, and the African flave-trade was thought moft advantageous for them, to enable themfelves to live in eafe and affluence by the cruel fubjection and flavery of others. The French and Englifh, and fome other nations in Europe, as they founded fettlements and colonies in the Weft Indies. or in America, went on in the fame manner, and joined hand in hand with the Portuguefe and Spaniards, to rob and pillage Africa, as well as to wafte and defolate the inhabitants of the weftern continent. But the European depredators and pirates have not only robbed and pillaged the people of Africa themfelves; but, by their inftigation, they have infefted the inhabitants with fome of the vileft combinations of fraudulent and treacherous villains, even among their own people; and have fet up their forts and factories as a refervoir of public and abandoned thieves, and as a den of defperadoes, where they may enfnare, entrap and catch men. So that Africa has been robbed of its inhabitants; its free-born fons and daughters have been ftole, and kidnapped, and violently taken away, and carried into captivity and cruel bondage. And it may be faid, in refpect to that diabolical traffic which is ftill carried on by the European depredators, that Africa has fuffered as much and more than any other quarter of the globe. O merciful God! when will the wickednefs of man have an end?

The

The Royal African Company (as is is called, ought rather to be reverfed as unworthy of the name) was incorporated 14th Charles II and impowered to trade from Salle in South Barbary to the Cape of Good Hope, and to erect forts and factories on the weftern eoaft of Africa for that purpofe. But this trade was laid open by an act of parliament, Anno 1697, and every private merchant permitted to trade thither, upon paying the fum of ten pounds towards maintaining the forts and garrifons. This Company, for fecuring their commerce, erected feveral factories on the coaft; the moft remarkable are thefe, viz. on the North part of Guinea, James Fort, upon an ifland in the River Gambia, Sierra Leona, and Sherbro; and on the South part of Guinea, viz. on the Gold Coaft, Dick's Cove, Succunda, Commenda, Cape Coaft Caftle, Fort Royal, Queen Anne's Point, Charles Fort, Annamabo, Winebah, Shidoe, Acra, &c. In all thefe places it is their grand bufnefs to traffic in the human fpecies; and dreadful and fhocking as it is to think, it has even been eftablifhed by royal authority, and is ftill fupported and carried on under a Chriftian government; and this muft evidently appear thereby, that the learned, the civilized, and even the enlightened nations are become as truly barbarous and brutifh as the unlearned.

To give any juft conception of the barbarous traffic carried on at thofe factories, it would be out of my power to defcribe the miferable fituation of the poor exiled Africans, which by the craft of wicked men daily become their prey, though I have feen enough of their mifery as well as read; no defcription can give an adequate idea

idea of the horror of their feelings, and the dreadful calamities they undergo. The treacherous, perfidious and cruel methods made ufe of in procuring them, are horrible and fhocking. The bringing them to the fhips and factories, and fubjecting them to brutal examinations ftripped naked and markings, is barbarous and bafe. Tne ftowing them in the holds of the fhips like goods of burden, with clofenefs and ftench, is deplorable; and, what makes addition to this deplorable fituation, they are often treated in the moft barbarous and inhuman manner by the unfeeling monfters of Captains. And when they arrive at the deftined port in the colonies, they are again ftripped naked for the brutal examination of their purchafers to view them, which, to many, muft add fhame and grief to their other woe, as may be evidently feen with forrow, melancholy and defpair marked upon their countenances. Here again another fcene of grief and lamentation arifes;—friends and near relations muft be parted never to meet again, nor knowing to whence they go. Here daughters are clinging to their mothers, and mothers to their daughters, bedewing each others naked breafts with tears; here fathers, mothers, and children, locked in each others arms, are begging never to be feparated; here the hufband will be pleading for his wife, and the wife praying for her children, and entreating, enough to melt the moft obdu rate heart, not to be torn from them, and taken away from her hufband; and fome will be ftill weeping for their native fhore, and their dear relations and friends, and other endearing connections which they have left behind, and have been barbaroufly tore away from, and all are
bemoaning

bemoaning themſelves with grief and lamentation at the proſpect of their wretched fate. And when ſold and delivered up to their inhuman purchaſers, a more heart-piercing ſcene cannot well take place. The laſt embrace of the beloved huſband and wife may be ſeen, taking their dear offspring in their arms, and with the moſt parental fondneſs, bathing their cheeks with a final parting endearment. But on this occaſion they are not permitted to continue long, they are ſoon torn away by their unfeeling maſters, entirely deſtitute of a hope of ever ſeeing each other again; and no conſolation is afforded to them in this ſorrowful and truly pitiable ſituation. Should any of them ſtill linger, and cling together a little longer, and not part as readily as their owners would have them, the flogger is called on, and they are ſoon drove away with the bloody commiſeration of the cutting fangs of the whip laſhing their naked bodies. This laſt exerciſe of the bloody whip, with many other cruel puniſhments, generally becomes an appendage of their miſerable fate, until their wretched lives be wore out with hunger, nakedneſs, hard labour, dejection and deſpair. Alas! alas! poor unhappy mortal! to experience ſuch treatment from men that take upon themſelves the ſacred name of Chriſtians!

In ſuch a vaſt extended, hideous and predominant ſlavery, as the Europeans carry on in their Colonies, ſome indeed may fall into better hands, and meet with ſome commiſeration and better treatment than others, and a few may become free, and get themſelves liberated from that cruel and galling yoke of bondage; but what are theſe to the whole, even hundreds of thouſands, held

and

and perpetrated in all the prevalent and intolerable calamities of that state of bondage and exile. The emancipation of a few, while ever that evil and predominant bufinefs of flavery is continued, cannot make that horrible traffic one bit the lefs criminal.   For, according to the methods of procuring flaves in Africa, there muft be great robberies and murders committed before any emancipation can take place, and before any lenitive favours can be fhewn to anv of them, even by the generous and humane.   This muft evidence that the whole of that bafe traffic is an enormous evil and wicked thing, which cries aloud for redrefs, and that an immediate end and ftop fhould be put to it.

The worthy and judicious author of the Hiftorical account of Guinea, and others, have given fome very ftriking eftimates of the exceeding evil occafioned by that wicked diabolical traffic of the African flave-trade; wherein it feems, of late years, the Englifh have taken the lead, or the greateft part of it, in carrying it on.   They have computed, that the fhips from Liverpool, Briftol and London have exported from the coaft of Africa upwards of one hundred thoufand flaves annually; and that among other evils attending this barbarous inhuman traffic, it is alfo computed that the numbers which are killed by the treacherous and barbarous methods of procuring them, together with thofe that perifh in the voyage, and die in the feafoning, amount to at leaft an hundred thoufand, which perifh in every yearly attempt to fupply the colonies, before any of the wretched furvivers, reduced to about fixty thoufand, annually required as an additional ftock can be made ufeful.   But as the great feverities and

H   oppreffions

oppreffions loaded upon the wretched furvivors
are fuch that they are continually wearing out,
and a new annual fupply wanted; that the vaft
carnage, and the great multitude of human fouls
that are actually deprived of life by carrying on
that iniquitous bufinefs, may be fuppofed to be
even more than one hundred thoufand that perifh
annually; or fuppofing that to be greatly lefs
than it is, ftill it is fo great that the very idea is
fhocking to conceive, at the thought of it fenfibility would blufh, and feeling nature abfolutely
turn pale.

" Gracious God! how wicked, how beyond all
" example impious, muft be that fervitude which
" cannot be carried on without the continual
" murder of fo many innocent perfons. What
" punifhment is not to be expected from fuch
" monftrous and unparalleled barbarity? For if
" the blood of one man unjuftly fhed cries with
" fo loud a voice for the Divine vengeance, how
" fhall the cries and groans of an hundred thou-
" fand men annually murdered afcend the celef-
" tial manfions, and bring down that punifhment
" fuch enormities deferve?" As this enormous
iniquity is not conjecture, but an obvious fact,
occafioned by that dreadful and wicked bufinefs
of flavery, were the inhabitants of Great-Britain
to hear tell of any other nation that murdered
one hundred thoufand innocent people annually,
they would think them an exceeding inhuman,
barbarous, and wicked people indeed, and that
they would be furely punifhed by fome fignal
judgment of Almighty God. But furely law and
liberty, juftice and equity, which are the proper foundations of the Britifh government, and
humanity the moft amiable characteriftic of the
                                              people,

people, muft be entirely fled from their land, if
they can think a lefs punifhment due to themfelves, for fupporting and carrying on fuch enormous wickednefs, if they do not fpeedily relin-
quifh and give it up. The very nature of that
wickednefs of enflaving of men is fuch, that were
the traffic, which European nations carry on in
it, a thoufand times lefs than it is, it would be
what no righteous nation would admit of for the
fake of any gain whatfoever. Wherefore as it is,
what ought to be done? If there is any righteoufnefs, any wifdom, any juftice, or any humanity
to be found, ought not the whole of it, and all
the branches of fuch exceeding evil and wicked
traffic, and all the iniquity of it to be relinquifh-
ed, and root and branches to be fpeedily given
up and put an end to?

   " For while fuch monftrous iniquity, fuch de-
" liberate barbarity and cruelty is carried on,
" whether it be confidered as the crime of indi-
" viduals, or as patronized and encouraged by
" the laws of the land, it holds forth an equal
" degree of enormity. And a crime founded in
" fuch a dreadful pre-eminence in wickednefs,
" both of individuals and the nation, muft fome
" time draw down upon them the heavieft judg-
" ments of Almighty God."—" On this occafion
" there feems already to be an interference of
" Divine Providence, though the obdurate and
" impenitent part of mankind may not regard it.
" The violent and fupernatural agitations of all
" the elements, which for a feries of years have
" prevailed in thofe European fettlements where
" the unfortunate Africans are retained in a ftate
" of flavery, and which have brought unfpeak-
" able calamities to the inhabitants, and public

" loffes

" loffes to the ftates to which they feverally be-
" long, are fo many awful vifitations of God for
" this inhuman violation of his laws. And it is
" not perhaps unworthy of remark, that as the
" fubjects of Great-Britain have two-thirds of this
" impious commerce in their own hands, fo they
" have fuffered in the fame proportioh, or more
" feverely than the reft. How far thefe misfor-
" tunes may appear to be acts of Providence, and
" to create an alarm to thofe who have been ac-
" cuftomed to refer every effect to its apparent
" caufe; who have been habituated to ftop there,
" and to overlook the finger of God, becaufe it
" is flightly covered under the veil of fecondary
" laws, we will not pretend to determine; but
" this we will affert with confidence, that the
" Europeans have richly deferved them all : the
" fear of fympathy that can hardly be reftrained
" on other melancholy occafions, feems to forget
" to flow at the relation of thefe ; and that we
" can never, with any fhadow of juftice, wifh
" profperity to the undertakers of thofe whofe
" fuccefs muft be at the expence of the happinefs
" of millions of their fellow-creatures *."

For though this world is not the place of final
retribution, yet there is an evidence maintained
in the courfe of Divine Providence, that verily
there is a God that judgeth in the earth. That

* See the excellent Mr. Clarkfon's Effay on the Slavery
and Commerce of the Human Species ; and, I muft add, the
amiable and indefatigable friend of mankind, Granville
Sharp, Efq; from whofe writings I have borrowed fome of
the following obfervations. I am alfo indebted to feveral
others, whofe intrinfic virtues will equally fhine in the fame
amiable manner, while ever there is any virtue and humanity amongft men ; and when thofe of the enflavers of men
will fink into abhorrence for ever.

nations may continue long, with a confiderable
degree of worldly profperity, and without feeming to be diftinguifhed by remarkable calamities.
when their wickednefs is become very great and
prevalent; yet it is no way inconfiftent to affert,
(and what facred hiftory warrant us to conclude)
that their judgment flumbereth not. Had one
been among the Canaanites a few years before the
Ifraelites entered their country, or in Babylon a
little before Cyrus encamped againft it, he would
have beheld a people in a ftate of great worldly
profperity, and in much fecurity, notwithftanding that the judgments of God were ready to
feize upon them. Great and deftructive wars are
kindled up from time to time, whereby multitudes of mankind are fwept away from the face
of the earth, and the wealth of nations are ex-
haufted. Famine, peftilence and earthquakes
have often fpread terror, defolation and mifery
among the inhabitants of the world. Nor are
there wanting inftances of remarkable national
diftreffes as a judgment for their wickednefs, by
a variety of other caufes. Though men cannot
eafily be prevailed with to regard thefe as the
operation of the hand of God, the fcriptures,
which contain the rules and hiftory of Divine Providence, reprefent thefe as inflicted for the fins of
nations, and not merely as cafual things, for
which no account can be given. And therefore
fome of thefe caufes which may feem natural,
and which have begun to make their appearance,
and the annual deftructions thereof which are
conftantly heard of in fome part or other, may
be confidered as tokens of God's judgments
againft the Britifh empire, and a variety of them
might be named; fuch as lofs of territory and

deftructive

deftructive wars, earthquakes and dreadful thun-
ders, ftorms and hurricanes, blaftings and deftructive infects, inclement and unfruitful feaions,
national debt and oppreffions, poverty and diftreffes of individuals, &c. *For his own iniquity
fhall take the wicked himfelf*; and who can tell
what dreadful calamities may yet befal to a people
refponfible for fo great a fhare of iniquity as in
that part which they carry on of the African
flave-trade alone. "And it is not known how
"foon a juft national retribution of vengeance
"may burft forth againft it; how foon the Al-
"mighty may think fit to recompence the Bri-
"tifh nation, according to the work, ot their
"hands, for the horrible oppreffion of the poor
"Africans.

"For national wickednefs from the beginning
"of the world has generally been vifited with
"national punifhments; and furely no national
"wickednefs can be more heinous in the fight of
"God than a public toleration of flavery, and
"fooner or later thefe kingdom will be vifited
"with fome fignal mark of his difpleafure, for
"the notorious oppreffion of the poor Africans,
"that are haraffed and continually wearing out
"with a moft fhameful involuntary fervitude in
"the Britifh colonies, and by a public toleration
"under the fanction of laws, to which the mo-
"narchs of England from time to time, by ad-
"vice of their privy counfellors, have given the
"royal affent, and thereby rendered themfelves
"parties in the oppreffion, and it may be feared
"partakers in their guilt."—"And every man
"has ample reafon to fear that God will make
"of this nation, in proportion to the magnitude
"of its guilt in the flave-dealing, a tremendous
"example

" example of retribution to deter other nations
" from offending his eternal juſtice, if a ſincere
" and ſpeedy repentance does not avert it."—
" For ſuch notorious crimes the Almighty, even
" the Lord, hath ſworn, *ſurely I will never forget*
" *any of theſe works.*" See Amos viii. But the
judgments of God are often ſuſpended and miti-
gated for the ſake of the righteous; and nations
are preſerved from deſtruction in favour to them
who remain faithful in times of general defection.
Iſaiah i. 9. " *Except the Lord of Hoſts had left us a*
" *very ſmall remnant, we ſhould have been as So-*
" *dom, and we ſhould have been like unto Go-*
" *morah.*"

But while ever ſuch a horrible buſineſs as the
ſlavery and oppreſſion of the Africans is carried
on, there is not one man in all Great-Britain and
her colonies, that knoweth any thing of it, can
be innocent and ſafe, unleſs he ſpeedily riſeth
up with abhorrence of it in his own judgment,
and, to avert evil, declare himſelf againſt it, and
all ſuch notorious wickedneſs. But ſhould the
contrary be adhered to, as it has been in the moſt
ſhameful manner, by men of eminence and power; according to their eminence in ſtation, the
nobles and ſenators, and every man in office and
authority, muſt incur a double load of guilt, and
not only that burden of guilt in the oppreſſion
of the African ſtrangers, but alſo in that of an
impending danger and ruin to their country;
and ſuch a double load of iniquity muſt reſt upon
thoſe guilty heads who withhold their teſtimony
againſt the crying ſin of tolerating ſlavery. The
inhabitants in general who can approve of ſuch
inhuman barbarities, muſt themſelves be a ſpecies
of unjuſt barbarians and inhuman men. But the
clergy

clergy of all denominations, whom we would consider as the devout messengers of righteousness,
peace, and good-will to all men, if we find any
of them ranked with infidels and barbarians, we
must consider them as particularly responsible;
and, in some measure, guilty of the crimes of
other wicked men in the highest degree. For it
is their duty to warn every man, and to teach
every man to know their errors; and if they do
not, the crimes of those under their particular
charge must rest upon themselves, and upon
some of them, in such a case as this, that of the
whole nation in general; and those (whatever
their respective situation may be) who forbid
others to assist them, must not be very sensible
of their own duty, and the great extensiveness
and importance of their own charge. And as it
is their great duty to teach men righteousness and
piety; this ought to be considered as sufficiently
obvious unto them, and to all men, that nothing
can be more contrary unto it, than the evil and
very nature of enslaving men, and making merchandize of them like the brute creation. " For
" it is evident that no custom established among
" men was ever more impious; since it is con-
" trary to reason, justice, nature, the principles
" of law and government, and the whole doc-
" trine, in short, of natural religion, and the re-
" vealed voice of God. And, therefore, that it
" is both evident and expedient, that there is an
" absolute necessity to abolish the slave trade, and
" the West-India slavery; and that to be in power,
" and to neglect even a day in endeavouring to
" put a stop to such monstrous iniquity and aban-
" doned wickedness (as the tenure of every man's
" life, as well as the time of his being in office
                                                    " and

" and power is very uncertain) muft neceffarily
" endanger a man's own eternal welfare, be he
" ever fo great in temporal dignity."

The higher that any man is exalted in power
and dignity, his danger is the more eminent,
though he may not live to fee the evil that may
eventually be contributed to his country, becaufe
of his difobedience to the law and commandments
of God. All men in authority, and kings in general, who are exalted to the moft confpicuous
offices of fuperiority, while they take upon themfelves to be the adminiftrators of righteoufnefs
and juftice to others, they become equally refponfible for admitting or fuffering others under their
authority to do wrong. Wherefore the higheft
offices of authority among men, are not fo defirable as fome may be apt to conceive; it was fo
confidered by the virtuous queen Anne, when fhe
was called to the royal dignity, as fhe declared to
the council of the nation, that it was a heavy
weight and burden brought upon her. For kings
are the minifters of God, to do juftice, and not to
bear the fword in vain, but to revenge wrath upon
them that do evil. But if they do not in fuch a
cafe as this, the cruel oppreffions of thoufands,
and the blood of the murdered Africans who are
flain by the fword of cruel avarice, muft reft upon
their own guilty heads in as eventually and plain
a fenfe as it was David that murdered Uriah; and
therefore they ought to let no companies of infidious merchants, or any guileful infinuations of
wicked men, prevail upon them to eftablifh
laws of iniquity, and to carry on a trade of oppreffion and injuftice; but they ought to confider
fuch as the worft of foes and rebels, and greater
enemies than any that can rife up againft their
temporal

temporal dignity. From all such enemies, good Lord, deliver them! for it is even better to lose a temporal kingdom, than only to endanger the happiness and enjoyment of an eternal one.

Nothing else can be conceived, but that the power of infernal wickedness has so reigned and pervaded over the enlightened nations, as to infatuate and lead on the great men, and the kings of Europe, to promote and establish such a horrible traffic of wickedness as the African slave trade and the West-India slavery, and thereby to bring themselves under the guilty responsibility of such awful iniquity. The kings and governors of the nations in general have power to prevent their subjects and people from enslaving and oppressing others, if they will ; but if they do not endeavour to do it, even if they could not effect that good purpose, they must then be responsible for their crimes; how much more, if they make no endeavours towards it, even when they can, and where no opposition, however plausible their pretences might be, would dare to oppose them. Wherefore, if kings or nations, or any men that dealeth unjustly with their fellow-creatures, to ensnare them, to enslave them, and to oppress them, or suffer others to do so, when they have it in their power to prevent it, and yet they do not, can it ever be thought that God will be well pleased with them? For can those which have no mercy on their fellow-creatures, expect to find mercy from the gracious Father of Men? Or will it not rather be said unto them, as it is declared, *that he who leadeth into captivity, shall be carried captive, and be bound in the cords of his own iniquity : Though hand join in hand the wicked shall not go unpunished: for sin and wickedness is the destruction of any people.*

And

And should these nations, in the most obnoxious and tenacious manner, still adhere to it as they have done, and continue to carry on in their colonies such works and purposes of iniquity, in oppression and injustice against the Africans, nothing else can be expected for them at last, but to meet with the fierce wrath of Almighty God, for such a combination of wickedness, according to all the examples of his just retribution, who cannot suffer such deliberate, such monstrous iniquity to go long unpunished.

There is good reason to suppose, that it was far from the intention of Ferdinand, king of Spain, to use his new subjects in America in the brutal and barbarous manner that his people did; and happy for the credit of that nation, and the honor of mankind, even among the profligate adventurers which were sent to conquer and desolate the new world, there were some persons that retained some tincture of virtue and generosity, and some men of the greatest reputation of both gentlemen and clergy, which did not only remonstrate, but protest against their measures then carried on. And since that iniquitous traffic of slavery has commenced and been carried on, many gentlemen of the most distinguished reputation, of different nations, and particularly in England, have protested and remonstrated against it. But the guileful insinuations of avaricious wicked men, which prevailed formerly, have still been continued; and to answer the purposes of their own covetousness, the different nations have been fomented with jealousy to one another, least another should have the advantage in any traffic; and while naturally emulous to promote their own ambition, they have imbrewed their hands in that
infamous

infamous commerce of iniquity; and by the infidious inftigation of thofe whofe private emolument depends on it, the various profligate adventurers, from time to time, have acquired the fanction of laws to fupport them, and have obtained the patronage of kings in their favour to encourage them, whereby that commerce of the moft notorious injuftice, and open violation of the laws of God, hath been carried on exceedingly to the fhame of all the Chriftian nations, and greatly to the difgrace of all the monarchs of Europe. The fact fpeaks itfelf: *And deftruction fhall be to the workers of iniquity.* The bold and oftenfive enflavers of men, who fubject their fellow-creatures to the rank of a brute, and the immolate value of a beaft, are themfelves the moft abandoned flaves of infernal wickednefs, the moft obnoxious ruffians among men, the enemies of their country, and the difgrace of kings. Their iniquity is wrote in the light as with a fun-beam, and engraven on the hardeft rock as with the point of a diamond, that cannot be eafily wiped away : *But the wicked fhall fall by their own wickednefs.* And, neverthelefs, by the infidious inftigations of thofe who have forfaken the amiable virtues of men, and have acquired the cruel ferocity of tygers and wild beafts, they have not only polluted themfelves with their iniquity, but their bafe treachery has brought fhame and guilt upon fome of the moft exalted and moft amiable characters in the world. And, therefore, that no evil may happen unto thofe who have been fo fhamefully beguiled and betrayed by the vile inftigations of wicked, profligate, inhuman men, and that no fhame and guilt may reft upon him, who ftandeth in the greateft eminence of refponfibility, I would ever

desire

defire to pray; let all the prayers of the wife and pious be heard for the king, and for his wife counfellors, and the great men that ftand before him; for kings and great men ftand in the moft perilous fituation of having the crimes of others imputed to them; wherefore kings have need of all your prayers, that the counfel of the wicked may not prevail againft them, for thefe are the worft foes, and moft terrible enemies, both to yourfelves and to your fovereign. *Righteouf-nefs exalteth a nation, but fin is a reproach to any people.*

In this advanced æra, when the kings of Europe are become more confpicuous for their manly virtues, than any before them have been, it is to be hoped that they will not any longer fuffer themfelves to be impofed upon, and be beguiled, and brought into guilt and fhame, by any inftigations of the cunning craftinefs and evil policy of the avaricious, and the vile profligate enflavers of men. And as their wifdom and underftanding is great, and exalted as their high dignity, it is alfo to be hoped that they will exert themfelves, in the caufe of righteoufnefs and juftice, and be like the wifeft and the greateft monarchs of old, to hearken to the counfel of the wife men that know the times, and to the righteous laws of God, and to deliver the oppreffed, and to put an end to the iniquitous commerce and flavery of men. And as we hear tell of the kings of Europe having almoft abolifhed, the infernal invention of the bloody tribunal of the inquifition, and the Emperor and others making fome grand reformations for the happinefs and good of their fubjects; it is to be hoped alfo that thefe exalted and liberal principles will lead them

on

on to greater improvements in civilization and felicitation, and next to abolish that other diabolical invention of the bloody and cruel African slave-trade, and the West-Indian slavery.

But whereas the people of Great-Britain having now acquired a greater share in that iniquitous commerce than all the rest together, they are the first that ought to set an example, left they have to repent for their wickedness when it becomes too late; left some impending calamity should speedily burst forth against them, and left a just retribution for their enormous crimes, and a continuance in committing similar deeds of barbarity and injustice should involve them in ruin. For we may be assured that God will certainly avenge himself of such heinous transgressors of his law, and of all those planters and merchants, and of all others, who are the authors of the Africans graves, severities, and cruel punishments, and no plea of any absolute necessity can possibly excuse them. And as the inhabitants of Great-Britain, and the inhabitants of the colonies, seem almost equally guilty of the oppression, there is great reason for both to dread the severe vengeance of Almighty God upon them, and upon all such notorious workers of wickedness; for it is evident that the legislature of Great-Britain patronises and encourages them, and shares in the infamous profits of the slavery of the Africans. It is therefore necessary that the inhabitants of the British nation should seriously consider these things for their own good and safety, as well as for our benefit and deliverance, and that they may be sensible of their own error and danger, left they provoke the vengeance of the Almighty against them. For what wickedness was there ever risen up so

monstrous,

monſtrous, and more likely to bring a heavy rod
of deſtruction upon a nation, than the deeds committed by the Weſt-Indian ſlavery, and the African ſlave trade. And even in that part of it carried on by the Liverpool and Briſtol merchants,
the many ſhocking and inhuman inſtances of
their barbarity and cruelty are ſuch, that every one
that heareth thereof has reaſon to tremble, and
cry out, *Should not the land tremble for this, and
every one mourn that dwelleth therein?*

The vaſt carnage and murders committed by
the Britiſh inſtigators of ſlavery, is attended
with a very ſhocking, peculiar, and almoſt un-
heard of conception, according to the notion of
the perpetrators of it; they either conſider them
as their own property, that they may do with
as they pleaſe, in life or death; or that the
taking away the life of a black man is of no more
account than taking away the life of a beaſt. A
very melancholy inſtance of this happened about
the year 1780, as recorded in the courts of law;
a maſter of a veſſel bound to the Weſtern Colonies, ſelected 132 of the moſt ſickly of the black
ſlaves, and ordered them to be thrown overboard
into the ſea, in order to recover their value from
the inſurers, as he had perceived that he was too
late to get a good market for them in the Weſt-
Indies. On the trial, by the counſel for the
owners of the veſſel againſt the underwriters,
their argument was, that the ſlaves were to be
conſidered the ſame as horſes; and their plea for
throwing them into the ſea, was nothing better
than that it might be more neceſſary to throw
them overboard to lighten their veſſel than goods
of greater value, or ſomething to that effect.
Theſe poor creatures, it ſeems, were tied two and

two

two together when they were thrown into the fea, left fome of them might fwim a little for the laft gafp of air, and, with the animation of their approaching exit, breath their fouls away to the gracious Father of fpirits. Some of the laft parcel, when they faw the fate of their companions, made their efcape from tying by jumping overboard, and one was faved by means of a rope from fome in the fhip. The owners of the veffel, I fuppofe, (inhuman connivers of robbery, flavery, murder and fraud) were rather a little defeated in this, by bringing their villainy to light in a court of law ; but the inhuman monfter of a captain was kept out of the way of juftice from getting hold of him. Though fuch perpetrators of murder and fraud fhould have been fought after from the Britifh Dan in the Eaft-Indies, to her Beerfhebah in the Weft.

But our lives are accounted of no value, we are hunted after as the prey in the defart, and doomed to deftruction as the beafts that perifh. And for this, fhould we appeal to the inhabitants of Europe, would they dare to fay that they have not wronged us, and grievoufly injured us, and that the blood of millions do not cry out againft them ? And if we appeal to the inhabitants of Great-Britain, can they juftify the deeds of their conduct towards us ? And is it not ftrange to think, that they who ought to be confidered as the moft learned and civilized people in the world, that they fhould carry on a traffic of the moft barbarous cruelty and injuftice, and that many, even among them, are become fo diffolute, as to think flavery, robbery and murder no crimes ? But we will anfwer to this, that no man can, with impunity. fteal, kidnap, buy or fell another man,

without

without being guilty of the moſt atrocious villainy. And we will aver, that every ſlave-holder that claims any property in ſlaves, or holds them in an involuntary ſervitude, are the moſt obnoxious and diſſolute robbers among men; and that they have no more right, nor any better title to any one of them, than the moſt profligate and notorious robbers and thieves in the world, has to the goods which they have robbed and ſtole from the right owners and lawful poſſ ſſor thereof. But ſhould the ſlave-holders ſay that they buy them; their title and claim is no better then that of the moſt notorious conniver, who buys goods from other robbers, knowing them to be ſtole, and accordingly gives an inferior price for them. According to the laws of England, when ſuch connivers are diſcovered, and the property of others unlawfully found in their poſſeſſion; the right owners thereof can oblige the connivers to reſtore back their property, and to puniſh them for their treſpaſs. But the ſlave-holders, univerſally, are thoſe connivers, they do not only rob men of ſome of their property, but they keep men from every property belonging to them, and compel them to their involuntary ſervice and drudgery ; and thoſe whom they buy from other robbers, and keep in their poſſeſſion, are greatly injured by them when compared to any ſpecies of goods whatſoever; and accordingly they give but a very inferior price for men, as all their vaſt eſtates in the Weſt-Indies is not ſufficient to buy one of them, if the rightful poſſeſſor was to ſell himſelf to them in the manner that they claim poſſeſſion of him. Therefore let the inhabitants of any civilized nation determine, whether, if they were to be treated in the ſame manner that

I   the

the Africans are, by various pirates, kidnappers, and flave-holders, and their wives, and their fons and daughters were to be robbed from them, or themfelves violently taken away to a perpetual and intolerable flavery; or whether they would not think thofe robbers, who only took away their property, lefs injurious to them than the other. If they determine it fo, as reafon muft tell every man, that himfelf is of more value than his property; then the executors of the laws of civilization ought to tremble at the inconfiftency of paffing judgment upon thofe whofe crimes, in many cafes, are lefs than what the whole legiflature muft be guilty of, when thofe of a far greater is encouraged and fupported by it wherever flavery is tolerated by law, and, confequently, that flavery can no where be tolerated with any confiftency to civilization and the laws of juftice among men; but if it can maintain its ground, to have any place at all, it muft be among a fociety of barbarians and thieves, and where the laws of their fociety is, for every one to catch what he can. Then, when theft and robbery becomes no crimes, the man-ftealer and the conniving flave-holder might poffibly get free.

But the feveral nations of Europe that have joined in that iniquitous traffic of buying, felling and enflaving men, muft in courfe have left their own laws of civilization to adopt thofe of barbarians and robbers, and that they may fay to one another, *When thou fawest a thief, then thou confentest with him, and haft been partaker with all the workers of iniquity.* But whereas every man, as a rational creature, is refponfible for his actions, and he becomes not only guilty in doing evil himfelf,

himfelf, but in letting others rob and opprefs
their fellow-creatures with impunity, or in not
delivering the oppreffed when he has it in his
power to help them. And likewife that nation
which may be fuppofed to maintain a very
confiderable degree of civilization juftice and
equity within its own jurifdiction, is not in
that cafe innocent, while it beholds another
nation or people carrying on perfecution, oppreffion and flavery, unlefs it remonftrates a-
gainft that wickednefs of the other nation, and
makes ufe of every effort in its power to help
the oppreffed, and to refcue the innocent. For
fo it ought to be the univerfal rule of duty to all
men that fear God and keep his commandments,
to do good to all men wherever they can; and
when they find any wronged and injured by
others, they fhould endeavour to deliver the enfnared whatever their grievances may be; and
fhould this fometimes lead them into war they
might expect the protection and bleffing of heaven. How far other motives may appear eligible
for men to oppofe one another with hoftile force,
it is not my bufinefs to enquire. But I fhould
fuppofe the hardy veterans who engage merely
about the purpofes of envying one another concerning any different advantages of commerce,
or for enlarging their territories and dominions,
or for the end of getting riches by their conqueft; that if they fall in the combat, they muft
generally die, as the fool dieth, vaunting in vain
glory; and many of them be like to thofe who
go out in darknefs, never to fee light; and
fhould they come off alive, what more does
their honour and fame amount to, but only to
be like that antediluvian conqueror, *who had*

flain

flain a man to his own wounding, and a young man to his hurt. But thofe mighty men of renown in the days of old, becaufe of their apoftacy from God, and rebellion and wickednefs to men, were at laft all fwallowed up by an nniverfal deluge for their iniquity and crimes.

But again let me obferve, that whatever civilization the inhabitants of Great-Britain may enjoy among themfelves, they have feldom maintained their own innocence in that great duty as a Chriftian nation towards others; and I may fay, with refpect to their African neighbours, or to any other wherefover they may go by the way of commerce, they have not regarded them at all. And when they faw others robbing the Africans, and carrying them into captivity and flavery, they have neither helped them, nor oppofed their oppreffors in the leaft. But inftead thereof they have joined in combination againft them with the reft of other profligate nations and people, to buy, enflave and make merchandize of them, becaufe they found them helplefs and fit to fuit their own purpofe, and are become the head carriers on of that iniquitous traffic. But the greater that any reformation and civilization is obtained by any nation, if they do not maintain righteoufnefs, but carry on any courfe of wickednefs and oppreffion, it makes them appear only the more inconfiftent, and their tyranny and oppreffion the more confpicuous. Wherefore becaufe of the great wickednefs, cruelty and injuftice done to the Africans, thofe who are greateft in the tranngreffion give an evident and undubious warrant to all other nations beholding their tyranny and injuftice to others, if thofe nations have any regard to their own innocence and virtue,

tue, and wifh to maintain righteoufnefs, and to
remain clear of the oppreffion and blood of all
men ; it is their duty to chaftize and fupprefs fuch
unjuft and tyrannical oppreffors and enflavers of
men. And fhould none of thefe be found among
the enlightened and civilized nations, who maintain their own innocence and righteoufnefs, with
regard to their duty unto all men ; and that
there may be none to chaftize the tyrannical
oppreffors of others ; then it may be feared, as
it has often been, that fierce nations of various
infects, and other annoyances, may be fent as a
judgment to punifh the wicked nations of men.
For by fome way or other every criminal nation,
and all their confederates, who fin and rebel
againft God, and againft his laws of nature and
nations, will each meet with fome awful retribution at laft, unlefs they repent of their iniquity.
And the greater advantages of light, learning,
knowledge and civilization that any people enjoy, if they do not maintain righteoufnefs, but do
wickedly, they will meet with the more fevere
rebuke when the vifitations of God's judgment
cometh upon them. And the prophecy which
was given to Mofes, is ftill as much in force
againft the enlightened nations now for their
wickednefs, in going after the abominations of
heathens and barbarians, for none elfe would attempt to enflave and make merchandize of men,
as it was when denounced againft the Ifraelitifh
nation of old, when they departed, or fhould
depart, from the laws and ftatutes of the Moft
High. *The Lord fhall bring a nation againft thee,
from far, from the ends of the earth, as fwift as
the eagle flieth, a nation whofe tongue thou fhalt not
underftand,* &c. See Deut. xxviii.

But

But left any of thefe things fhould happen to the generous and refpectuful Britons, who are not altogether loft to virtue and confideration; let me fay unto you, in the language of a wife and eminent Queen, as fhe did when her people were fold as a prey to their enemies: That it is not all your enemies (for they can be reckoned nothing elfe), the covetous inftigators and carriers on of flavery and wickednefs, that can in any way countervail the damage to yourfelves, to your king, and to your country; nor will all the infamous profits of the poor Africans avail you any thing if it brings down the avenging hand of God upon you. We are not faying that we have not finned, and that we are not deferving of the righteous judgments of God againft us. But the enemies that have rifen up againft us are cruel, oppreffive and unjuft; and their haughtinefs of infolence, wickednefs and iniquity is like to that of Haman the fon of Hammedatha; and who dare fuppofe, or even prefume to think, that the inhuman ruffians and enfnarers of men, the vile negociators and marchandizers of the human fpecies, and the oftenfive combinations of flavt-holders in the Weft have done no evil? And fhould we be paffive, as the fuffering martyrs dying in the flames, whofe blood crieth for vengeance on their perfecutors and murderers; fo the iniquity of our oppreffors, enflavers and murderers rife up againft them. For we have been hunted after as the wild beafts of the earth, and fold to the enemies of mankind as their prey; and fhould any of us have endeavoured to get away from them, as a man would naturally fly from an enemy that way-laid him; we have been purfued after, and, by haughty mandates and laws

laws of iniquity, overtaken, and murdered and
flain, and the blood of millions cries out againſt
them. And together with theſe that have been
cruelly ſpoiled and flain, the very grievous af-
flictions that we have long ſuffered under, has
been long crying for vengeance on our oppreſſors ; and the great diſtreſs and wretchedneſs
of human woe and miſery, which we are yet
lying under, is ſtill riſing up before that High
and Sovereign Hand of Juſtice, where men, by
all their oppreſſion and cruelty, can no way prevent ; their evil treatment of others may ſerve to
increaſe the blow, but not to evade the ſtroke of
His power, nor withhold the bringing down that
arm of vengeance on themſelves, and upon all
their connivers and confederators, and the particular inſtigators of ſuch wilful murders and
inhuman barbarity. The life of a black man is
of as much regard in the fight of God, as the life
of any other man ; though we have been ſold as
a carnage to the market, and as a prey to profligate wicked men, to torture and laſh us as they
pleaſe, and as their caprice may think fit, to murder us at diſcretion.

And ſhould any of the beſt of them plead, as
they generally will do, and tell of their humanity
and charity to thoſe whom they have captured
and enſlaved, their tribute of thanks is but ſmall ;
for what is it, but a little reſtored to the wretched
and miſerable whom they have robbed of their
all ; and only to be dealt with, like the ſpoils of
thoſe taken in the field of battle, where the
wretched fugitives muſt ſubmit to what they
pleaſe. For as we have been robbed of our natural right as men, and treated as beaſts, thoſe
who have injured us, are like to them who have
                                        robbed

robbed the widow, the orphans, the poor and the needy of their right, and whofe children are rioting on the fpoils of thofe who are begging at their doors for bread. And fhould they fay, that their fathers were thieves and connivers with enfnarers of men, and that they have been brought up to the iniquitous practice of flavery and oppreffion of their fellow-creatures, and they cannot live without carrying it on, and making their gain by the unlawful merchandize and cruel flavery of men, what is that to us, and where will it juftity them? And fome will be faying, that the Black people, who are free in the Weft Indies, are more miferable than the flaves;—and well they may; for while they can get their work and drudgery done for nothing, it is not likely that they will employ thofe whom they muft pay for their labour. But whatever neceffity the enflavers of men may plead for their iniquitous practice of flavery, and the various advantages which they get by it can only evidence their own injuftice and difhonefty. A man that is truly honeft, fears nothing fo much as the very imputation of injuftice; but thofe men who dare not face the confequence of acting uprightly in every cafe are deteftable cowards, unworthy the name of men; for it is manifeft that fuch men are more afraid of temporal inconveniencies than they are of God: *And I fay unto you, my friends, be not afraid of them that kill the body, and after that have no more that they can do; but I will forewarn you whom you fhall fear: Fear him, who, after he hath killed, hath power to caft into hell.* Luke xii. 4, 5.

But why fhould a total abolition, and an univerfal emancipation of flaves, and the enfranchifement of all the Black People employed in the culture

ture of the Colonies; taking place as it ought to
do, and without any hesitation, or delay for a
mom nt, even though it might have some seem-
ing appearance of loss either to government or to
individuals, be feared at all? Their labour, as
freemen, would be as useful in the sugar colonies
as any other class of men that could be found;
and should it even take place in such a manner
that some individuals, at first, would suffer loss
as a just reward for their wickedness in slave-
dealing, what is that to the happiness and good
of doing justice to others ; and, I must say, to the
great danger, otherwise, that must eventually
hang over the whole community ? It is certain,
that the produce of the labour of slaves, together
with all the advantages of the West-India traffic,
bring in an immense revenue to government ; but
let that amount be what it will, there might be
as much or more expected from the labour of an
equal increase of free people, and without the im-
plication of any guilt attending it, and which,
otherwise, must be a greater burden to bear, and
more ruinous consequences to be feared from it,
than if the whole national debt was to sink at once,
and to rest upon the heads of all that might suffer
by it. Whereas, if a generous encouragement
were to be given to a free people, peaceable
among themselves, intelligent and industrious,
who by art and labour would improve the most
barren situations, and make the most of that
which is fruitful ; the free and voluntary labour
of many, would soon yield to any government,
many greater advantages than any thing that slavery can produce. And this should be expected,
wherever a Christian government is extended,
and the true religion is embraced, that the blessings

fings of liberty fhould be extended likewife, and that it fhould diffufe its influences firft to fertilize the mind, and then the effects of its benignity would extend, and arife with exuberant bleffings and advantages from all its operations. Was this to be the cafe, every thing would increafe and profper at home and abroad, and ten thoufand times greater and greater advantages would arife to the ftate, and more permanent and folid bene-fit to individuals from the fervice of freemen, than ever they can reap, or in any poffible way enjoy, by the labour of flaves.

But why this diabolical traffic of flavery has not been abolifhed before now, and why it was introduced at all, as I have already enquired, muft be greatly imputed to that powerful and pervading agency of infernal wickednefs, which reigneth and prevaileth over the nations, and to that umbrageous image of iniquity eftablifhed thereby; for had there been any truth and right-eoufnefs in that grand horn of delufion in the eaft, which may feem admirable to fome, and be look-ed upon by its votaries as the fine burnifhed gold, and bright as the fineft polifhed filver, then would not flavery, cruelty and oppreffion have been abo-lifhed wherever its influence came? And had the grand apoftacy of its fellow horn, with all its li-neaments been any better, and endowed with any real virtue and goodnefs, whom its devotees may behold as the fineft polifhed diamond, and glif-tening as the fineft gems, then would not flavery and barbarity have been prohibited and forbidden wherever the beams of any Chriftianity arofe? Then might we have expected to hear tidings of good, even from thofe who are gone to repofe in the fabulous paradife of Mahomet?
Then

Then might we have looked for it from thofe
who are now reclined to flumber in affimulation
with the old dotards of Rome, or to thofe who
are fallen afleep and become enamoured with the
fcarlet couch of the abominable enchantrefs dyed
in blood ? And as well then might we not expect
tendernefs and compaffion from thofe whom the
goddefs of avarice has fo allured with her charms,
that her heart-fick lovers are become reverfed to
the feelings of human woe; and with the great
hurry and buftle of the ruffet flaves employed in
all the drudgeries of the weftern ifles, and mari-
time fhore, in the cruel and involuntary fervice
of her voluptuoufnefs, having fo dazzled their
eyes, and bereaved them of all fenfibility, that
their hearts are become callous as the nether mill-
ftone, fierce as the tygers, and devoid of the natural feelings of men? From all fuch enchant-
ments we would turn away, and fly from them as
from the ravenous beafts of prey, as from the
weeping crocodiles and the devouring reptiles,
and as from the hoary monfters of the deep.

But we would look unto you, O ye multitude
in the defart! againft whom there is no enchant-
ment, neither any divination whatever, that can
prevail againft you! for in your mouth there is
no error or guile to be found, nor any fault before the throne of God. And what! though
your dwellings be in all lands, and ye have no
nation or kingdom on earth that ye can call
your own, and your camp be furrounded with
many enemies, yet you have a place of defence,
an invincible fortrefs, the munitions of rocks for
your refuge, and the fhield of your anointed is
Almighty; and behold his buckler is ftrong, and
his fceptre is exalted on high, and the throne
of

of his dominion and power ruleth over all. But in the day that we fhall be fpoken for, if we find you a wall, we would build upon you a palace of filver; and if you find us a door, inclofe us with boards of cedar, for we long, and would to God that we longed more, to enter into your fortrefs, and follow you to your happy retreat. Then might we, like you, ftand undaunted before our foes, and with more than heroic fullennefs at all their cruel tortures, highly difdain their rage, and boldly dare them to do their worft. For you, O ye friends of the Moft High, when you die, when ye are perfecuted and flain, when you fall in the combat, when you die in the battle, it is you! only you, that come off conquerors, and more than conquerors through him that loved you! And fhould it yet be, as it has often been, that your foes might purfue you with their ufual arrogance and perfecuting rage, and caufe you to die cruelly veiled in a curtain of blood, lo! your ftains are all wafhed away, and your wounds and fcars will foon be healed, and yourfelves will be then invefted with a robe of honor that will fhine in whitenefs for ever new, and your blood that was fhed by the terrific rage of your foes, will teftify againft them, and rife up in grandeur to you, as an enfringement of gold floating in glory, and as his robe of honor which flames in eternal crimfon through the heavens. But we envy no man, but wifh them to do good, and not evil; and we want the prayers of the good, and where-ever they can to help us; and the blefling of God be with all the promoters of righteoufnefs and peace.

But wherefore, O beloved, fhould your watch-men fit ftill, when they hear tell that the enemy is invading all the out-pofts and camp of the Bri-

tifh

tifh empire, where many of your dwellings are?
Are they all fallen afleep, and lying down to flumber in affimilation with the workers of iniquity?
Should not thofe who are awake, arife, and give
the alarm, that others may arife and awake alfo?
And fhould not they who feareth the name of the
Lord, and worfhip in his holy temples, *Let judgment to run down as waters, and righteoufnefs as a
mighty ftream?* But why think ye prayers in
churches and chapels only will do ye good, if
your charity do not extend to pity and regard
your fellow creatures perifhing through ignorance, under the heavy yoke of fubjection and
bondage, to the cruel and avaricious oppreffion of
brutifh profligate men; and when both the injured, and their oppreffors, dwell in fuch a vicinity
as equally to claim your regard? The injurers,
oppreffors, enflavers, and murderers of others,
eventually bring a curfe upon themfelves, as far
as they deftroy, injure, and cruelly and bafely
treat thofe under their fubjection and unlawful
bondage. And where fuch a dreadful pre-eminence of iniquity abounds, as the admiffion of
laws for tolerating flavery and wickednefs, and
the worft of robberies, not only of men's properties, but themfelves; and the many inhuman
murders and cruelties occafioned by it: If it
meets with your approbation, it is your fin, and
you are then as a conniver and confederator with
thofe workers of wickednefs; and if you give it a
fanction by your paffive obedience, it manifefts
that you are gone over to thofe brutifh enemies
of mankind, and can in no way be a true lover of
your king and country.

Wherefore it ought to be the univerfal endeavour, and the ardent wifh, of all the lovers of
God

God and the Saviour of men, and of all that delight in his ways of righteoufnefs, and of all the
lovers of their country, and the friends of mankind, and of every real patriot in the land, and
of every man and woman that dwelleth therein,
and of all thofe that have any pretence to charity, generofity, fenfibility and humanity, and
whoever has any regard to innocence and virtue,
to plead that flavery, with all its great and heinous magnitude of iniquity, might be abolifhed
throughout all the Britifh dominions; and from
henceforth to hinder and prohibit the carrying on
of that barbarous, brutifh and inhuman traffic
of the flavery and commerce of ·the human fpecies, wherever the power and influence of the
Britifh empire extends. And in doing this, and
always in doing righteoufly, let the glory and honour of it be alone afcribed unto God Moft High,
for his great mercy and goodnefs to you; and
that his bleffings and unbounded beneficence may
fhine forth upon you, and upon all the promoters
of it : and that it may with great honours and
advantages of peace and profperity be ever refting upon the noble Britons, and upon their moft
worthy, moft eminent and auguft Sovereign, and
upon all his government and the people under it ;
and that the ftreams thereof may run down in
righteoufnefs even to us, poor deplorable Africans.

And we that are particularly concerned would
humbly join with all the reft of our brethren and
countrymen in complexion, who have been grievoufly injured, and who jointly and feparately,
in all the language of grief and woe, are humbly imploring and earneftly entreating the moft
refpectful and generous people of Great Britain,
that they would confider us, and have mercy and
compaffion

compaſſion on us, and to take away that evil that your enemies, as well as our oppreſſors, are doing towards us, and cauſe them to deſiſt from their evil treatment of the poor and deſpiſed Africans, before it be too late; and to reſtore that juſtice and liberty which is our natural right, that we have been unlawfully deprived and cruelly wronged of, and to deliver us from that captivity and bondage which we now ſuffer under, in our preſent languiſhing ſtate of exile and miſery. And we humbly pray that God may put it into the minds of the noble Britons, that they may have the honor and advantage of doing ſo great good to many, and to extend their power and influence to do good afar; and that great good in abundance may come down upon themſelves, and upon all their government and the people under it, in every place belonging to the Britiſh empire. But if the people and the legiſlature of Great-Britain altogether hold their peace at ſuch a time as this, and even laugh at our calamity as heretofore they have been wont to do, by making merchandize of us to enrich themſelves with our miſery and diſtreſs: we ſit like the mourning Mordecai's at their gates cloathed in ſackcloth; and, in this advanced era, we hope God in his Providence will riſe up a deliverance for us ſome other way; and we have great reaſon to hope that the time of our deliverance is faſt drawing nigh, and when the great Babylon of iniquity will fall.

And whereas we conſider our caſe before God of the whole univerſe, the Gracious Father and Saviour of men; we will look unto him for help and deliverance. The cry of our affliction is already gone up before him, and he will hearken

to

to the voice of our diſtreſs; for he hears the cries and groans of the oppreſſed, and profeſſes that if they cry at all unto him, he will hearken unto them, and deliver them. *For the oppreſſion of the poor, for the ſighing of the needy, now will I ariſe ſaith Jehovah, and will ſet him in ſafety from him that puffeth at him, or that would enſnare him.* (Pſa. xii. 5.) *And I know that Jehovah will maintain the cauſe of the afflicted, and the right of the poor.* (Pſa. cxl. 12.) Wherefore it is our duty to look up to a greater deliverer than that of the Britiſh nation, or of any nation upon earth; for unleſs God gives them repentance, and peace towards him, we can expect no peace or deliverance from them. But ſtill we ſhall have cauſe to truſt, that God who made of one blood all the nations and children of men, and who gave to all equally a natural right to liberty; that the who ruleth over all the kingdoms of the earth with equal providential juſtice, ſhall then make enlargement and deliverance to ariſe to the grievouſly injured, and heavy oppreſſed Africans from another place.

And as we look for our help and ſure deliverance to come from God Moſt High, ſhould it not come in an apparent way from Great-Britain, whom we conſider as the Queen of nations, let her not think to eſcape more than others, if ſhe continues to carry on oppreſſion and injuſtice, and ſuch pre-eminent wickedneſs againſt us: for we are only ſeeking that juſtice may be done to us, and what every righteous nation ought to do; and if it be not done, it will be adding iniquity to iniquity againſt themſelves. But let us not ſuppoſe that the inhabitants of the Britiſh nation will adhere to the ways of the profligate.: *For ſuch is*
the

the way of an adulterous woman; she eateth, and wipeth her mouth; and saith, I have done no wickedness. But rather let us suppose, *That whereas iniquity hath abounded, may righteousness much more abound.* For the wickedness that you have done is great, and wherever your traffic and colonies have been extended it is shameful; and the great injustice and cruelty done to the poor Africans crieth to heaven against you; and therefore that it may be forgiven unto you, it cries aloud for universal reformation and national repentance. But let it not suffice that a gracious call from the throne is inviting you, *To a religious observance of God's holy laws, as fearing, left God's wrath and indignation, should be provoked against you;* but in your zeal for God's holy law, because of the shameful transgression thereof, every man every woman hath reason to mourn apart, and every one that dwelleth in the land ought to mourn and sigh for all the abominations done therein, and for the great wickedness carried on thereby.

And now that blessings may come instead of a curse, and that many beneficent purposes of good might speedily arise and flow from it, and be more readily promoted: I would hereby presume to offer the following considerations, as some outlines of a general reformation which ought to be established and carried on. And first, I would propose, that there ought to be days of mourning and fasting appointed, to make enquiry into that great and pre-eminent evil for many years past carried on against the Heathen nations, and the horrible iniquity of making merchandize of us, and cruelly enslaving the poor Africans: and that you might seek grace and repentance, and find mercy and forgiveness before God Omnipotent; and that he may give

K   you

you wifdom and underftanding to devife what ought to be done.

Secondly, I would propofe that a total abolition of flavery fhould be made and proclaimed; and that an univerfal emancipation of flaves fhould begin from the date thereof, and be carried on in the following manner: That a proclamation fhould be caufed to be made, fetting forth the Antichriftian unlawfulnefs of the flavery and commerce of the human fpecies; and that it fhould be fent to all the courts and nations in Europe, to require their advice and affiftance, and as they may find it unlawful to carry it on, let them whofoever will join to prohibit it. And if fuch a proclamation be found advifable to the Britifh legiflature, let them publifh it, and caufe it to be publifhed, throughout all the Britifh empire, to hinder and prohibit all men under their government to traffic either in buying or felling men; and, to prevent it, a penalty might be made againft it of one thoufand pounds, for any man either to buy or fell another man. And that it fhould require all flave-holders, upon the immediate information thereof, to mitigate the labour of their flaves to that of a lawful fervitude, without tortures or oppreffion; and that they fhould not hinder, but caufe and procure fome fuitable means of inftruction for them in the knowledge of the Chriftian religion. And agreeable to the late *royal Proclamation, for the Encouragement of Piety and Virtue, and for the preventing and punifhing of Vice, Profanenefs and Immorality;* that by no means, under any pretence whatfoever, either for themfelves or their mafters, the flaves under their fubjection fhould not be fuffered to work on the Sabbath days, unlefs it be fuch works as neceffity and

and mercy may require. But that thofe days, as well as fome other hours felected for the purpofe, fhould be appropriated for the time of their inftruction; and that if any of their owners fhould not provide fuch fuitable inftructors for them, that thofe flaves fhould be taken away from them and given to others who would maintain and inftruct them for their labour. And that it fhould be made known to the flaves, that thofe who had been above feven years in the iflands or elfewhere, if they had obtained any competent degree of knowledge of the Chriftian religion, and the laws of civilization, and had behaved themfelves honeftly and decently, that they fhould immediately become free; and that their owners fhould give them reafonable wages and maintenance for their labour, and not caufe them to go away unlefs they could find fome fuitable employment elfewhere. And accordingly, from the date of their arrival to feven years, as they arrive at fome fuitable progrefs in knowledge, and behaved themfelves honeftly, that they fhould be getting free in the courfe of that time, and at the end of feven years to let every honeft man and woman become free; for in the courfe of that time, they would have fufficiently paid their owners by their labour, both for their firft purpofe, and for the expences attending their education. By being thus inftructed in the courfe of feven years, they would become tractable and obedient, ufeful labourers, dutiful fervants and good fubjects; and Chriftian men might have the honor and happinefs to fee many of them vieing with themfelves to praife the God of their falvation. And it might be another neceffary duty for Chriftians, in the courfe of that time, to

K 2   make

make enquiry concerning some of their friends and relations in Africa : and if they found any intelligent persons amongst them, to give them as good education as they could, and find out a way of recourse to their friends ; that as soon as they had made any progress in useful learning and the knowledge of the Christian religion, they might be sent back to Africa, to be made useful there as soon, and as many of them as could be made fit for instructing others. The rest would become useful residentors in the colonies ; where there might be employment enough given to all free people, with suitable wages according to their usefulness, in the improvement of land ; and the more encouragement that could be given to agriculture, and every other branch of useful industry, would thereby encrease the number of the inhabitants ; without which any country, however blessed by nature, must continue poor.

And, thirdly, I would propose, that a fleet of some ships of war should be immediately sent to the coast of Africa, and particularly where the slave trade is carried on, with faithful men to direct that none should be brought from the coast of Africa without their own consent and the approbation of their friends, and to intercept all merchant ships that were bringing them away, until such a scrutiny was made, whatever nation they belonged to. And, I would suppose, if Great-Britain was to do any thing of this kind, that it would meet with the general approbation and assistance of other Christian nations ; but whether it did or not, it could be very lawfully done at all the British forts and settlements on the coast of Africa ; and particular remonstrances could be

given

given to all the rest, to warn them of the confequences of fuch an evil and enormous wicked traffic as is now carried on. The Dutch have fome crocodile fettlers at the Cape, that fhould be called to a particular account for their murders and iuhuman barbarities. But all the prefent governors of the Britifh forts and factories fhould be difmiffed, and faithful and good men appointed in their room ; and thofe forts and factories, which at prefent are a den of thieves, might be turned into fhepherd's tents, and have good fhepherds fent to call the flocks to feed befide them. Then would doors of hofpitality in abundance be opened in Africa to fupply the weary travellers, and that immenfe abundance which they are enriched with, might be diffufed afar ; but the character of the inhabitants on the weft coaft of Africa, and the rich produce of their country, have been too long mifreprefented by avaricious plunderers and merchants who deal in flaves ; and if that country was not annually ravifhed and laid wafte, there might be a very confiderable and profitable trade carried on with the Africans. And, fhould the noble Britons, who have often fupported their own liberties with their lives and fortunes, extend their philanthropy to abolifh the flavery and oppreffion of the Africans, they might have fettlements and many kingdoms united in a friendly alliance with themfelves, which might be made greatly to their own advantage, as well as they might have the happinefs of being ufeful to promoting the profperity and felicity of others, who have been cruelly injured and wrongfully dealt with. Were the Africans to be dealt with in a friendly manner, and kind inftruction to be adminiftered unto them, as by

K 3　　　　　degrees

degrees they became to love learning, there would be nothing in their power, but what they would wifh to render their fervice in return for the means of improving their underftanding; and the prefent Britifh factories, and other fettlements, might be enlarged to a very great extent. And as Great-Britain has been remarkable for ages paft, for encouraging arts and fciences, and may now be put in competition with any nation in the known world, if they would take compaffion on the inhabitants of the coaft of Guinea, and to make ufe of fuch means as would be needful to enlighten their minds in the knowledge of Chriftianity, their virtue, in this refpect, would have its own reward. And as the Africans became refined and eftablifhed in light and knowledge, they would imitate their noble Britifh friends, to improve their lands, and make ufe of that induftry as the nature of their country might require, and to fupply thofe that would trade with them, with fuch productions as the nature of their climate would produce; and, in every refpect, the fair Britons would have the preference with them to a very great extent; and, in another refpect, they would become a kind of firft ornament to Great-Britain for her tender and compaffionate care of fuch a fet of diftreffed poor ignorant people. And were the noble Britons, and their auguft Sovereign, to caufe protection and encouragement to be given to thofe Africans, they might expect in a fhort time, if need required it, to receive from thence great fupplies of men in a lawful way, either for induftry or defence; and of other things in abundance, from fo great a fource, where every thing is luxurious and plenty, if not laid wafte by barbarity and grofs ignorance.

Due

Due encouragement being given to fo great, fo juft, and fuch a noble undertaking, would foon bring more revenue in a righteous way to the Britifh nation, than ten times its fhare in all the profits that flavery can produce * ; and fuch a laudable example would infpire every generous and enterprizing mind to imitate fo great and worthy a nation, for eftablifhing religion, juftice, and equity to the Africans, and, in doing this, would be held in the higheft efteem by all men, and be admired by all the world.

Thefe three preceding confiderations may fuffice at prefent to fhew, that fome plan might be adopted in fuch a manner as effectually to relieve the grievances and oppreffion of the Africans, and to bring great honour and bleffings to that nation, and to all men whofoever would endeavour to promote fo great good to mankind ; and it might render more confpicuous advantages to the noble Britons, as the firft doers of it, and greater honour than the finding of America was at firft to thofe that made the difcovery : Though feveral difficulties may feem to arife at firft, and the good to be fought after may appear as remote and unknown, as it was to explore the unknown regions of the Weftern Ocean ;

* A gentleman of my acquaintance told me that, if ever he hears tell of any thing of this kind taking place, he has a plan in contemplation, which would, in fome equitable manner, produce from one million to fifteen millions fterling to the Britifh government annually, as it might be required ; of which a due proportion of that revenue would be paid by the Africans ; and that it would prevent all fmuggling and illicit traffic ; in a great meafure, prevent running into debt, long imprifonment, and all unlawful bankruptcies ; effectually prevent all difhonefty and fwindling, and almoft put an end to all robbery, fraud and theft.

fhould

should it be sought after, like the intrepid Columbus, if they do not find kingdoms of wealth by the way, they may be certain of finding treasures of happiness and peace in the end. But should there be any yet alive deserving the infamy and character of all the harsh things which I have ascribed to the insidious carriers on of the slavery and commerce of the human species, they will certainly object to any thing of this kind being proposed, or ever thought of, as doing so great a good to the base Black Negroes whom they make their prey. To such I must say again, that it would be but a just commutation for what cannot be fully restored, in order to make restoration, as far as could be, for the injuries already done to them. And some may say, that if they have wages to pay to the labourers for manufacturing the West-India productions, that they would not be able to sell them at such a price as would suit the European market, unless all the different nations agreed to raise the price of their commodities in proportion. Whatever bad neighbours men may have to deal with, let the upright shew themselves to be honest men, and that difficuly, which some may fear, would be but small, as there can be no reason for men to do wrong because others do so; but as to what is consumed in Great-Britain, they could raise the price in proportion, and it would be better to sip the West-India sweetness by paying a little more money for it (if it should be found needful) than to drink the blood of iniquity at a cheaper rate. I know several ladies in England who refuse to drink sugar in their tea, because of the cruel injuries done to the Black People employed in the culture of it at the West-Indies. But should it

cost

coft the Weft-Indians more money to have their manufactories carried by the labour of freemen than with flaves, it would be attended with greater bleffings and advantages to them in the end. What the wages fhould be for the labour of freemen, is a queftion not fo eafily determined; yet I fhould think, that it always ought to be fomething more than merely victuals and cloaths; and if a man works by the day, he fhould have the three hundredth part of what might be eftimated as fufficient to keep him in neceffary cloaths and provifions for a year, and, added to that, fuch wages of reward as their ufefulnefs might require. Something of this kind fhould be obferved in free countries, and then the price of provifions would be kept at fuch a rate as the induftrious poor could live, without being oppreffed and fcrewed down to work for nothing, but only barely to live. And were every civilized nation, where they boaft of liberty, fo ordered by its government, that fome general and ufeful employment were provided for every induftrious man and woman, in fuch a manner that none fhould ftand ftill and be idle, and have to fay that they could not get employment, fo long as there are barren lands enough at home and abroad fufficient to employ thoufands and millions of people more than there are. This, in a great meafure, would prevent thieves and robbers, and the labour of many would foon enrich a nation. But thofe employed by the general community fhould only have their maintenance either given or eftimated in money, and half the wages of others, which would make them feek out for fomething elfe whenever they could, and half a loaf would be better than no bread. The men that were employed

ployed in this manner, would form an useful militia, and the women would be kept from a state of misery and want, and from following a life of dissolute wickedness. Liberty and freedom, where people may starve for want, can do them but little good. We want many rules of civilization in Africa; but, in many respects, we may boast of some more essential liberties than any of the civilized nations in Europe enjoy; for the poorest amongst us are never in distress for want, unless some general and universal calamity happen to us. But if any nation or society of men were to observe the laws of God, and to keep his commandments, and walk in the way of righteousness, they would not need to fear the heat in sultry hot climates, nor the freezing inclemency of the cold, and the storms and hurricanes would not hurt them at all; they might soon see blessings and plenty in abundance showered down upon their mountains and vallies; and if his beneficence was sought after, who martials out the drops of the dew, and bids the winds to blow, and to carry the clouds on their wings to drop down their moisture and fatness on what spot soever he pleaseth, and who causeth the genial rays of the sun to warm and cherish the productions of the earth in every place according to that temperature which he sees meet; then might the temperate climes of Great-Britain be seen to vie with the rich land of Canaan of old, which is now, because of the wickedness of its inhabitants, in comparison of what it was, as only a barren desart.

Particular thanks is due to every one of that humane society of worthy and respectful gentlemen, whose liberality hath supported many of the Black

poor

poor about London. *Those that honor their Maker have mercy on the poor; and many blessings are upon the head of the just: may the fear of the Lord prolong their days, and cause their memory to be blessed, and may their number be encreased to fill their expectation with gladness;* for they have not only commiserated the poor in general, *but even those which are accounted as beasts, and imputed as vile in the sight of others.* The part that the British government has taken, to co-operate with them, has certainly a flattering and laudable appearance of doing some good; and the fitting out ships to supply a company of Black People with clothes and provisions, and to carry them to settle at Sierra Leona, in the West coast of Africa, as a free colony to Great-Britain, in a peaceable alliance with the inhabitants, has every appearance of honour, and the approbation of friends. According to the plan, humanity hath made its appearance in a more honorable way of colonization, than any Christian nation have ever done before, and may be productive of much good, if they continue to encourage and support them. But after all, there is some doubt whether their own flattering expectation in the manner as set forth to them, and the hope of their friends may not be defeated and rendered abortive; and there is some reason to fear, that they never will be settled as intended, in any permanent and peaceable way at Sierra Leona.

This prospect of settling a free colony to Great-Britain in a peaceable alliance with the inhabitants of Africa at Sierra Leona, has neither altogether met with the credulous approbation of the Africans here, nor yet been sought after with any prudent and right plan by the promoters of
it.

it. Had a treaty of agreement been firſt made with the inhabitants of Africa, and the terms and nature of ſuch a ſettlement fixed upon, and its ſituation and boundary pointed out; then might the Africans, and others here, have embarked with a good proſpect of enjoying happineſs and proſperity themſelves, and have gone with a hope of being able to render their ſervices, in return, of ſome advantage to their friends and benefactors of Great-Britain. But as this was not done, and as they were to be hurried away at all events, come of them after what would; and yet, after all, to be delayed in the ſhips before they were ſet out from the coaſt, until many of them have periſhed with cold, and other diſorders, and ſeveral of the moſt intelligent among them are dead, and others that, in all probability, would have been moſt uſeful for them were hindered from going, by means of ſome diſagreeable jealouſy of thoſe who were appointed as governors, the great proſpect of doing good ſeems all to be blown away. And ſo it appeared to ſome of thoſe who are now gone, and at laſt, hap hazard, were obliged to go; who endeavoured in vain to get away by plunging into the water, that they might, if poſſible wade aſhore, as dreading the proſpect of their wretched fate, and as beholding their perilous ſituation, having every proſpect of difficulty and ſurrounding danger.

What with the death of ſome of the original promoters and propoſers of this charitable undertaking, and the death and deprivation of others that were to ſhare the benefit of it, and by the adverſe motives of thoſe employed to be the conductors thereof, we think it will be more than what can be well expected, if we ever hear of of any good in proportion to so great, well-designed, laudable and expensive charity. Many more of the Black People still in this country would have, with great gladness, embraced the opportunity, longing to reach their native land; but as the old saying is, A burnt child dreads the fire, some of these unfortunate sons and daughters of Africa have been severally unlawfully dragged away from their native abodes, under various pretences, by the insidious treachery of others, and have been brought into the hands of barbarous robbers and pirates, and, like sheep to the market, have been sold into captivity and slavery, and thereby have been deprived of their natural liberty and property, and every connection that they held dear and valuable, and subjected to the cruel service of the hard-hearted brutes called planters. But some of them, by various services either to the public or to individuals, as more particularly in the course of last war, have gotten their liberty again in this free country. They are thankful for the respite, but afraid of being ensnared again; for the European seafaring people in general, who trade to foreign parts, have such a prejudice against Black People, that they use them more like asses than men, so that a Black Man is scarcely ever safe among them. Much assiduity was made use to persuade the Black People in general to embrace the opportunity of going with this company of transports; but the wiser sort declined from all thoughts of it, unless they could hear of some better plan taking place for their security and safety. For as it seemed prudent and obvious to many of them taking heed to that sacred enquiry, *Doth a fountain send forth at the same place sweet*

sweet water and bitter? They were afraid that their doom would be to drink of the bitter water. For can it be readily conceived that government would eftablifh a free colony for them nearly on the fpot, while it fupports its forts and garrifons, to enfnare, merchandize, and to carry others into captivity and flavery.

Above fifty years ago, P. Gordon, in his Geography, though he was no advocate againft flavery, complains of the barbarities committed againft the Heathen nations, and the bafe ufage of the negroe flaves fubjected to bondage as brutes, and deprived of religion as men. His remark on the religion of the American iflands, fays : " As for the negroe flaves, their lot has " hitherto been, and ftill is, to ferve fuch Chrif- " tian mafters, who fufficiently declare what " zeal they have for their converfion, by un- " kindly ufing a ferious divine fome time ago, " for only propofing to endeavour the fame." This was above half a century ago, and their un- chriftian barbarity is ftill continued. Even in the little time that I was in Grenada, I faw a flave receive twenty-four lafhes of a whip for being feen at a church on a Sunday, inftead of going to work in the fields ; and thofe whom they put the greateft confidence in, are often ferved in the fame manner. The noble propofals offered for inftructing the heathen nations and people in his Geography, has been attended to with great fupinenefs and indifference. The author wifhes, that " fincere endeavours might be made " to extend the limits of our Saviour's kingdom, " with thofe of our own dominions ; and to " fpread the true religion as far as the Britifh fails " have done for traffic." And he adds, " Let " our

" our planters duly confider, that to extirpate
" natives, is rather a fupplanting than planting a
" new colony ; and that it is far more honoura-
" ble to overcome paganifm in one, than to de-
" ftroy a thoufand pagans. Each convert is a
" conqueft."

To put an end to the nakednefs of flavery and
merchandizing of men, and to prevent murder,
extirpation and diffolution, is what every righteous nation ought to feek after ; and to endeavour
to diffufe knowledge and inftruction to all the heathen nations wherever they can, is the grand duty of all Chriftian men. But while the horrible
traffic of flavery is admitted and practiced, there
can be but little hope of any good propofals meeting with fuccefs anywhere ; for the abandoned carriers of it on have fpread the poifon of
their iniquity wherever they come, at home and
abroad. Were the iniquitous laws in fupport of
it, and the whole of that oppreffion and injuftice
abolifhed, and the righteous laws of Chriftianity,
equity, juftice and humanity eftablifhed in the
room thereof, multitudes of nations would flock
to the ftandard of truth, and inftead of revolting
away, they would count it their greateft happinefs to be under the protection and jurifdiction
of a righteous government. And in that refpect,
*in the multitude of the people is the King's honour ;
but in the want of people, is the deftruction of the
Prince.*

We would wifh to have the grandeur and fame
of the Britifh empire to extend far and wide ;
and the glory and honor of God to be promoted
by it, and the intereft of Chriftianity fet forth
among all the nations wherever its influence and
power can extend ; but not to be fupported by
the

the infidious pirates, depredators, murderers and flave-holders. And as it might diffufe know-ledge and inftruction to others, that it might receive a tribute of reward from all its territo-ries, forts and garrifons, without being oppref-five to any. But contrary to this the wickednefs of many of the White People who keep flaves, and contrary to all the laws and duties of Chrif-tianity which the Scriptures teach, they have in general endeavoured to keep the Black People in total ignorance as much as they can, which muft be a great difhonor to any Chriftian government, and injurious to the fafety and happinefs of rulers.

But in order to diffufe any knowledge of Chrif-tianity to the unlearned Heathens, thofe who un-dertake to do any thing therein ought to be wife and honeft men. Their own learning, though the more the better, is not fo much required as that they fhould be men of the fame mind and principles of the apoftle Paul ; men that would hate coveteoufnefs, and who would hazard their lives for the caufe and gofpel of our Lord and Saviour Jefus Chrift. " I think it needlefs to " to exprefs how commendable fuch a defign " would be in itfelf, and how defirable the pro-" motion thereof fhould be to all who ftile them-" felves Chriftians, of what party or profeffion " foever they are." Rational methods might be taken to have the Scriptures tranflated into many foreign languages ; " and a competent number " of young ftudents of theology might be edu-" cated at home in thefe foreign languages, to " afford a conftant fupply of able men, who " might yearly go abroad, and be fufficiently " qualified at their firft arrival to undertake the " great work for which they were fent." But

as

as a hindrance to this, the many Anti-chriſtian errors which are gone abroad into the world, and all the popiſh ſuperſtition and nonſenſe, and the various aſſimilations unto it, with the falſe philo-ſophy which abounds among Chriſtians, ſeems to threaten with an univerſal deluge; but God hath promiſed to fill the world with a knowledge of himſelf, and he hath ſet up his bow, in the ra-tional heavens, as well as in the clouds, as a token that he will ſtop the proud ways of error and de-luſion, that hitherto they may come, and no far-ther. The holy arch of truth is to be ſeen in the azure paths of the pious and wiſe, and conſpicu-ouſly painted in crimſon over the martyrs tombs. Theſe, with the golden altars of truth, built up by the reformed churches, and many pious, good and righteous men, are bulwarks that will ever ſtand againſt all the forts of error. Teaching would be exceeding neceſſary to the pagan na-tions and ignorant people in every place and ſituation; but they do not need any unſcriptural forms and ceremonies to be taught unto them; they can deviſe ſuperſtitions enough among them-ſelves, and church government too, if ever they need any.

And hence we would agree in this one thing with that erroneous philoſopher, who has lately wrote *An Apology for Negro Slavery*, "But if the "ſlave is only to be made acquainted with the "form, without the ſubſtance; if he is only to "be decked out with the external trappings of "religion; if he is only to be taught the un-"cheering principles of gloomy ſuperſtition; or, "if he is only to be inſpired with the intemperate "frenzy of enthuſiaſtic fanaticiſm, it were better "that he remained in that dark ſtate, where he "could not ſee good from ill." But theſe words

L   *intemperate,*

intemperate, frenzy, enthufiaftic, and *fanaticifm* may be variouſly applied, and often wrongfully ; but, perhaps never better, or more fitly, than to be aſcribed as the genuine character of this author's brutiſh philoſophy ; and he may ſubſcribe it, and the meaning of theſe words, with as much affinity to himſelf, as he bears a relation to a *Hume,* or to his friend *Tobin.* The poor negroes in the Weſt-Indies, have ſuffered enough by ſuch religion as the philoſophers of the North produce ; Proteſtants, as they are called, are the moſt barbarous ſlave-holders, and there are none can equal the Scotch floggers and negroe-drivers, and the barbarous Dutch cruelties. Perhaps as the church of Rome begins to ſink in its power, its followers may encreaſe in virtue and humanity ; ſo that many, who are the profeſſed adherents thereof, would even bluſh and abhor the very mention of the cruelty and bloody deeds that their anceſtors have committed ; and we find ſlavery itſelf more tolerable among them, than it is in the Proteſtant countries.

But I ſhall add another obſervation, which I am ſorry to find among Chriſtians, and I think it is a great deficiency among the clergy in general, when covetous and profligate men are admitted amongſt them, who either do not know, or dare not ſpeak the truth, but neglect their duty much, or do it with ſuch ſupineneſs, that it becomes good for nothing. Sometimes an old woman ſelling matches, will preach a better, and a more orthodox ſermon, than ſome of the clergy, who are only decked out (as Mr. Turnbul calls it) with the external trappings of religion. Much of the great wickedneſs of others lieth at their door, and theſe words of the Prophet are applicable to them : *And firſt, ſaith faith the Lord, I will recompence their iniquity, and their fin double; becaufe they have defiled my land, they have filled mine inheritance with the carcafes of their deteftable and abominable things.* Such are the errors of men. Church, fignifies an affembly of people; but a building of wood, brick or ftone, where the people meet together, is generally called fo; and fhould the people be frightened away by the many abominable dead carcafes which they meet with, they fhould follow the multitudes to the fields, to the vallies, to the mountains, to the iflands, to the rivers, and to the fhips, and compel them to come in, that the houfe of the Lord may be filled. But when we find fome of the covetous connivers with flave-holders, in the Weft-Indies, fo ignorant as to difpute whether a Pagan can be baptized without giving him a Chriftian name, we cannot expect much from them, or think that they will follow after much good. No name, whether Chriftian or Pagan, has any thing to do with baptifm; if the requifite qualities of knowledge and faith be found in a man, he may be baptized let his name be what it will. And Chriftianity does not require that we fhould be deprived of our own perfonal name, or the name of our anceftors; but it may very fitly add another name unto us, Chriftian, or one anointed. And it might as well be anfwered fo to that queftion in the Englifh liturgy, *What is your name?*—A Chriftian.

     " *A Chriftian is the higheft ftile of man!*
     " *And is there, who the bleffed crofs wipes off*
     " *As a foul blot, from his difhonor'd brow?*
     " *If angels tremble, 'tis at fuch a fight:*
     " *The wretch they quit difponding of their charge,*
     " *More ftruck with grief or wonder who can tell?*"

         And

And let me now hope that you will pardon me in all that I have been thus telling you, O ye inhabitants of Great-Britain! to whom I owe the greateſt reſpect; to your king! to yourſelves! and to your government! And tho' many things which I have written may ſeem harſh, it cannot be otherwiſe evaded when ſuch horible iniquity is tranſacted; and tho' to ſome what I have ſaid may appear as the rattling leaves of autumn, that may ſoon be blown away and whirled in a vortex where few can hear and know : I muſt yet ſay, although it is not for me to determine the manner, that the voice of our complaint implies a vengeance, becauſe of the great iniquity that you have done, and becauſe of the cruel injuſtice done unto us Africans; and it ought to ſound in your ears as the rolling waves around your circum-ambient ſhores; and if it is not hearkened unto, it may yet ariſe with a louder voice, as the rolling thunder, and it may encreaſe in the force of its volubility, not only to ſhake the leaves of the moſt ſtout in heart, but to rend the mountains before them, and to cleave in pieces the rocks under them, and to go on with fury to ſmite the ſtouteſt oaks in the foreſt; and even to make that which is ſtrong, and wherein you think that your ſtrength lieth, to become as ſtubble, and as the fibres of rotten wood, that will do you no good, and your truſt in it will become a ſnare of infatuation to you!

F I N I S.